Climbing Down

Graham Wilson

CLIMBING DOWN

with illustrations by Gerry Dale

Millrace

First published in Great Britain in 2002 by
Millrace
2a Leafield Road, Disley
Cheshire SK12 2JF

Reprinted November 2003

ISBN: 1 902173 120

Typeset in Baskerville BE Regular.
Printed and bound in Great Britain.

Acknowledgements

I would like to acknowledge Dave Hewitt's permission to use an extract from *Walking the Watershed* and his continued efforts to support the real rights of walkers. A rather different acknowledgement to Tricia, who sacrificed her right to walk at the rate she enjoyed to accommodate the peaks and troughs of my self-indulgent aspirations.

GPW

Contents

Preface

Now, infidel, I have thee on the hip.
(The Merchant of Venice)

It was not long after the publication of *Macc and the Art of Long Distance Walking* that I met a long standing acquaintance in a place of public refreshment. I knew that he had bought a copy of the book and I was trying to engineer the conversation in the direction of his purchase. Finesse having failed, I adopted the forthright approach and awaited the response. His brow furrowed.

To tell the truth, I was disappointed.

I waited for further elucidation but there was none forthcoming. We fell silent. The bar fell silent. Half a Lager Joe stirred, sensing an opportunity to join the conversation and conveniently catch hold of the coat tails of a round. The pause, however, had been for thought.

You see, it's not what I wanted or, I suppose, expected. The Art of Long Distance Walking – he seemed to weigh the words individually – *I have nothing against long distances as such. In fact, when I sort out the present little wrinkle* – he waved his hand with the air of a man constantly impeded by such unfortunate inconvenience – *I intend to put as much ... distance ... as possible between it and myself and, what is more* – another gesture probably indicating magnanimity – *I have always admired the idea of a marathon effort ever since I saw Scott and the Antarctic at the Picturedrome in nineteen whatever it was. No, I have nothing against long distance walking. It's walking long distances that I find* – he paused again – *a little pedestrian. You see, I thought that's what you meant by the 'Art'. You had discovered the secret of Long Distance Walking without walking long distances. Bliss without blisters, if you see what I mean.*

I saw what he meant and it had crossed my mind at the time of writing that I might try something along those lines but I had other matters to attend to that occupied my literary ambitions. In any event, the book had been born out of the training I had been doing for an attempt on the Bob Graham Round and a sponsored jog through the Lakeland fells from Coniston Old Man to Skiddaw and those days and companions were gone. What's more, I still felt that short walks in the Peak District, whilst pleasant enough, were not that much to write home about. Then something rather odd happened.

I was about to start Stage 3 of my thirty-year plan. The decided aims were not exclusive but were to form the core of my walking campaigns. Stage 1, in my forties, was to explore Scotland, with particular reference to the Munros; Stage 2 (fifties) to climb all the remaining 'interesting' mountains in Britain; and Stage 3 (sixties) to complete a series of long distance through-routes which, linked together, would form a continuous journey that meandered through the length and much of the breadth of the country. At the time of its conception this seemed a modest enough plan without unduly tempting fate. But, as I said, something odd happened.

As a starter to Stage 3 and to test tactics and temperament, we embarked on the Southern Upland Way, a well marked cross-country route, starting at Portpatrick and finishing two hundred and twelve miles later at Cockburnspath, and crossing in the process the whole of Scotland in an area between the border and the M8. I had sped through this marginal country on numerous occasions to reach the *real* Scottish hills, but felt perhaps the area deserved more than a cursory glance and the SUW would provide the opportunity. The route falls into twelve days of obvious but at times lengthy walking. Rather than bash straight across, we decided to divide it into four separate excursions and, while we were there, explore the towns and villages of Galloway and the Borders. As the area is comparatively well served by public transport, the plan was to leave the excess luggage at our eventual destination and then train/bus to the starting point of the section. After three days' walking, we would be reintroduced to clean socks and civilisation.

The first section includes a fair amount of road work and it was to this that I put down an ache in my left thigh. Section 2 is the crux of the walk. It crosses remote moorland and forestry from Bargrennan to Sanquhar and, as there are few stopping places that offer the opportunity to replenish the vital liquids, distances of twenty plus miles had to be accomplished in a day. After ten miles my left leg began to ache, after fifteen to hurt and I eventually limped into Dalry at what might be best described as a whimper. The four Bs (Bath, Beer, Bed & Breakfast) seemed to cure the problem and the next day went well until after ten miles, etc. Plans were hastily recast. Four sections became seven and, towards the end, twenty-four hours' rest was required between daily stages. I, who

4

had previously walked non-stop all day, ignoring piteous requests for a moment's pause to unwrap a Mars Bar, now trudged disconsolately in the wake of a companion newly secure in the knowledge that she could stop and prepare a three-course meal before the reduced male eventually caught up. It was not long into the day before I was left behind with the exhortation that *a stout troop of Girl Guides would be doing this in half the time* – or perhaps it was a troupe of stout Girl Guides. I really only caught glimpses of the words as I passed them hanging in the air.

Matters got worse. By Christmas, even a trip to the local was proving almost too much. The time had come for serious consideration. Earlier X-rays had proved inconclusive so I decided to burgle the NHS through the skylight of private consultation. Immediately all was revealed and I jumped ship to join the public queue waiting for a free hip replacement. Diagnosis is one thing; action is another. It is all very well for governments to proclaim the availability of free health for all at the point of delivery, but if the patient, when finally seen, is then past remedy, there seems little point of, or in, delivery at all. With regard to the treatment of defective joints, it seems that the alleviation of pain is given higher priority than returning flexibility of movement. In other words, unless you writhed in agony you would not be moved on to the operating list. Although this is understandable on humanitarian grounds, I feel it is rather shortsighted. Pressure on the Health Service in general might be lessened if the public were kept active and on its feet. In my experience, mooching around the house is conducive to neither physical nor mental health.

So, with a collapsing hip and the advent of Foot and Mouth, the mountain challenge disappeared into a metaphorical mist. As a result, it seemed as good a time as any to consider another walking book. The bonus was that I could meet up again with my illustrator, Gerry Dale. It was generally agreed that his drawings in *Macc & the Art,* with their mixture of cartography and charisma, gave much to the text. What is more, it was always a pleasure to discuss detail and watch him resolve the problem of producing long and complex routes in a single drawing. At the very least, it would give me the opportunity to recall past outings. If I couldn't walk the hills, I might, to some extent, relive them on the map. I was also delighted that the publishers, Millrace, were again keen to produce the volume as a proper book, *ie* hardback, sewn, dust jacket, etc. Books and mountains have given me much pleasure in life and to have the opportunity to bring them together is, to say the least, satisfactory.

I soon discovered another consequence of relative immobility. It is my habit to avoid driving if an alternative form of transport is available. This is not an attempt to cast myself as the saviour of the ozone layer but rather that I find traffic jams particularly irritating – I even dislike stopping for petrol. If you are sitting in a bus or train and it ceases to move, you can continue to read, write or fill in your football pools. In a car you can only fume or drop into a Radio One-induced coma. So, if I am annoyed by roads that are rapidly approaching gridlock, it would be a particularly foolish self-inflicted wound were I to contribute to the present mess. The simplest form of alternative transport is to walk and the network of existing footpaths connects most places that you would care to visit. It is, after all, usually the shortest way from A to B. As an example, I am writing this in Lyme Park. To travel from home to Lyme Hall by road is eleven miles of single carriageway which includes the horrendous A6. If I walk, it is eight miles which I can accomplish by setting foot on no more than a few hundred yards of tarmac. No great affair when I was fit but, as deterioration set in, walking distances were getting inexorably shorter and uneven ground became more difficult to negotiate at anything above snail's pace. As a result I was forced to investigate the local public transport system and found it more extensive and flexible than I had imagined.

The key is the *Wayfarer* concept. Both Greater Manchester PTA and Derbyshire County Council run such schemes and through them you can easily purchase a single ticket that covers any bus, train or tram journey on the same day. If you were to start at Buxton, for example, you could complete a mini-tour of the varied delights of the Peak District without undue exertion. A day out could be as follows:

Stage 1   Bus to Baslow through the villages of Tideswell and Eyam.

Stage 2   A walk along the gritstone edges of Baslow, Curbar and Froggatt, dropping through the Longshaw Estate to Grindleford Station.

Stage 3   Train through the Hope valley to Edale, where lunch is taken.

Stage 4   A traverse of Kinder Scout and Brown Knoll with a descent to Whaley Bridge via Buxworth.

Stage 5   Bus or train to Buxton.

The general idea behind the scheme has certain advantages. It allows the car to stay in the garage and encourages the use of public transport, which use in rural areas may well save it from extinction. Local buses may be slower but they often visit interesting places such as Eyam or Ashford-in-the-Water which have been bypassed in the all-consuming desire to move from one traffic jam to the next at the highest possible speed. Pleasure can be attained from planning the journey. The need to catch connections can give the expedition a certain momentum. If, through negligence or necessity, you find yourself in the wrong valley, your car would most probably be further away than the nearest bus stop. It is cheap – there are fare concessions for the old, young and families of two point four children. If anyone knows an alternative way to get from Bolton to Ashbourne or Macclesfield to Nottingham and back for less than four quid, I would be interested to hear from him. You can tailor the outing to suit your own needs and abilities. The suggested itinerary could be extended by starting the walk at Chatsworth, or shortened by taking Jacob's Ladder to Edale Cross and dropping into Hayfield. Provided you have the copies of the relevant timetables in your sack, you can chop and change as you wish or as the weather dictates.

Of all the bus journeys I made, the trip from Macclesfield to Buxton was the one that gave me most pleasure. Once the A537 has pulled out of the town, passing through a dappled tunnel of trees to the junction of the aptly named Cliff Lane, it cleverly holds its height above the sunken land of Wildboarclough and Danebower. It is only on the final pull to the summit that the engine breaks sweat and starts to tumble through the gears. After the Cat and Fiddle is passed, all that remains is the plunge off the rough edges of Axe Moor into the leafy gentility of spas and arias.

In between this rise and fall there is a clough-riven moorland invisible from either town. It is a secret world. Even Shutlingsloe, distinctive enough from certain angles to be christened The Matterhorn of the Peak, is rarely glimpsed from the plains. Only the Old Road, which cuts through the heart of the country in its uncompromising fashion, sees a little of what is really there. But the view from the box seat of the local bus service gives a fine introduction. It is best during the week. At weekends you will share the view with a surfeit of motorcyclists. They, too, are attracted by the elegant bends and the pitch and toss of the ride. Pageanted in aggressive leather and black-tinted perspex, they poise on machines that scatter the silence and to the uninitiated can appear a fearsome sight. But at the Cat and Fiddle, their summer gathering-ground, all is different. Once divested of their twentieth-century panoply, these Wild Ones seem less Marlon Brando, more retired Bank Manager.

That is not to say that there are no raptors about. At the final bends, the bus climbs above the general level of the land and looks down on the windhover eyeing its prey. For a moment or two we also are performers in this play within a play, watching Hamlet watching the Poisoner King. And not only kestrels: peregrine, as elsewhere, is becoming more prevalent and, to the annoyance of the racing fraternity, giving its own slant to the term pigeon fancier. But nothing *really* big; there's not sufficient rocky fastness. Though there is one point on the road where the humble rocks of Windgather appear less an edge than a promontory, not unlike the Hebridean Sgurr of Eigg. A fancy once given credence when slow-dispersing morning mist clung round it like the sea.

One advantage of this trip is that it is sufficiently short to be done at all times of the day and on most days in the year. This offers a variety of visual pleasures – gritstone walls snow-laced by a late spring flurry, the warmer hues of autumn, the suffused light of a summer's evening shading the softened contours. At times, winter overcomes the efforts of even the most determined entrepreneur. The road is closed and if you still feel the need for a pint of Robinson's Bitter at altitude, then, I'm afraid, you'll have to walk.

Another advantage is that the walker can alight at the Cat and Fiddle, the second highest pub in England, and continue on foot either back to Macclesfield or deeper into Derbyshire. Routes 1 (Virgin Territory) and 4 (Catabasis) follow this option. The first title refers to the bus formerly run by Virgin Trains from Macclesfield to Buxton and beyond. This was an excellent example of the rail/road link *service* that the present government professes to support. Lack of profitability caused its demise. However, Derbyshire and Cheshire County Councils have combined to produce a replacement service. The second title was a happy discovery. I was searching for a word that would anticipate the connection between the Cat and Fiddle and the Puss in Boots when I discovered the term 'Catabasis'. It not only means a downward journey, which reflects that chapter in particular and the book in general, but is also a medical term for the moment when an illness starts to decline, again appropriate as the outing was the first relatively serious undertaking after I had relearnt to walk. But that was in the future. Foot and Mouth had abated. If I was serious about trying to revisit old haunts, albeit propped up on my new trendy trekking pole, I had run out of excuses.

One
Virgin Territory

withering on the virgin thorn
(A Midsummer Night's Dream)

So I left the bus, or rather the bus left me, at the Cat and Fiddle. 10.30 am. All closed. Time to put theory into practice.

I intended to walk from the Cat to Whaley Bridge via Shining Tor and Taxal. It wasn't far and was for the most part downhill. If the hip refused to function, I could always roll. I had now added to my collection of 'useful things to take on a walk' a walking stick and a mobile phone. In this day of *à la mode* gear, where clothes seem to be held together mostly by zips, a walking stick is no longer anything so simple. It is now more grandly a Trek Pole. There was a time when we thought the Victorian mountaineers rather quaint as they posed outside their hotels clutching their alpenstocks. Now we are full circle, with all and sundry tooled up for their assault on the great outdoors, not to mention the *après-promenade* technical exchange. In fact, the pole with its extendable reach is very useful and can perform better service than the humble stick in fending off farm animals at large (particularly large) and dogs with dubious intentions.

Mobile phones are also intriguing. Like reading glasses, there is a tendency to leave them lying about, and they can often only be traced by the absurdity of ringing yourself. The case for the lone walker carrying such an instrument is incontrovertible and it was with this voice of reason ringing in my ears that I made enquiries at the appropriate outlet. The assistant was very knowledgeable and explained, in response to my efforts to develop the metaphor, that their phones did not 'ring' in the conventional sense but instead played a variety of tunes. He then proceeded, at length, to demonstrate. It was when he was half-way through explaining how to customise the menu that I mentioned I would only want it for emergencies and wondered if there were many parts of the UK that the system didn't cover. The assistant, as if dealing with a small but willing child, reached for the map. Only these, he indicated, explaining that they were not areas of real significance. As the insignificant areas consisted of the highlands of Britain, it appeared that the phone might all too soon join the

15

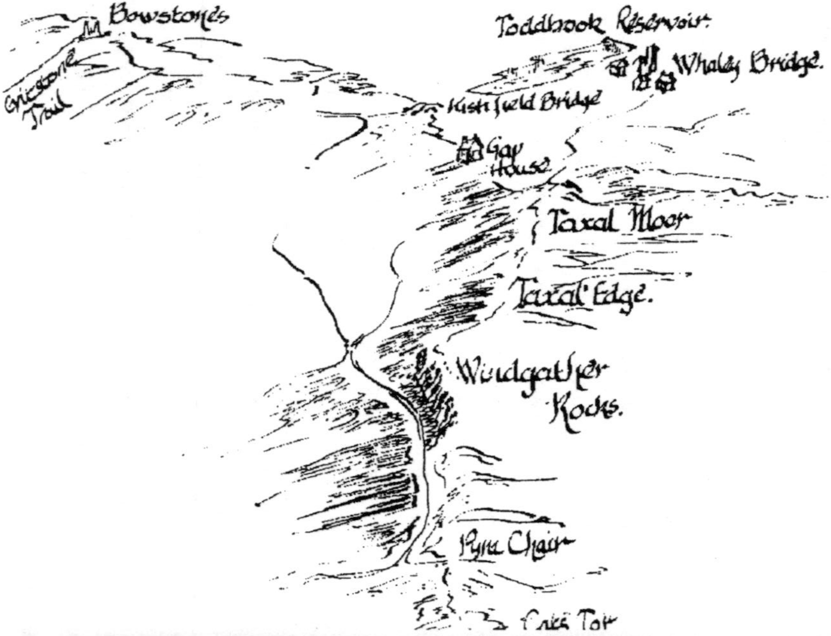

Bowstones

Oaken Clough
Cross

Toddbrook Reservoir

Whaley Bridge

Kettleshulme Bridge

Jay House

Taxal Moor

Taxal Edge

Windgather Rocks

Pym Chair

Cats Tor

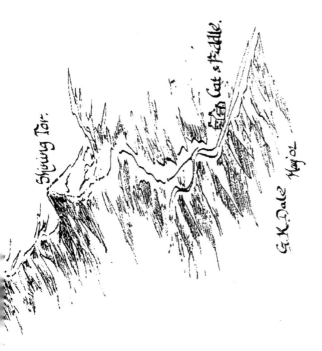

Shining Tor.

Cat & Fiddle.

G.K.Dale Major

Route One: Virgin Territory

other 'useful things' that hibernate in the bottom of my rucksack. Still, I am sure that not all is lost and that many a walker when demoralised by wind and rain has conjured the blood and stiffened the sinews by playing snatches of Wagner or the Overture to William Tell at moments of crisis.

The path to Shining Tor is broad and easy but I knew from memory that there were two stiles to be surmounted before reaching the summit. As with all *mauvais pas*, they were worse in contemplation than actuality. The inexperienced Trek Pole proved more of a hindrance than a help but, with the aid of an undignified scuttling, the hurdles were overcome. I now realised why the world is full of polite old gentlemen who, on approaching a stile or similar obstacle, stand back and insist you must go first. It was then I understood that, with my carbon fibre helpmate and double bows on my boots, I had slipped, as it were, over an edge.

Quite which edge I was not sure but through some related trickle of consciousness recalled Mark Twain's remarks on the ageing process. At the age of twenty he realised that his father knew little or nothing about the ways of the world. At the age of thirty, however, he was surprised how much the old man had learnt in the last ten years. Perhaps age, or slipping over the edge, does offer another perspective. Days no longer geared to linking as many tickable tops as possible might bring alternative pleasures. Finding time to stand and stare, inner contemplation – that type of thing. Mind you, if you believe that sort of guff, you might as well pack it in and take up golf.

Despite the distraction of such philosophical speculation, the ascent to the trig point seemed harder than usual. Was it the hip or the unfavourable diurnal ratio of pints to yards (litres to metres has a certain good old Common Market ring), where the former is in excess of what you would reasonably mention to your doctor and the latter is the shortest route to the Dog and Monkey? The top was reached and the gloom lifted by the sight of Shutlingsloe caught in a loop of sunlight, a fellow shining tor. There are moments in life when you smile both to and at yourself.

The ridge continues over Cat Tor and acts as an arm that enfolds another valley hidden from general view. At Pym Chair, you descend to an old Roman road, known locally as 'The Street'. There is much dispute as to who Pym was. Some say he was a preacher who, through fear of judicial retribution, was forced to use this out-of-the-way spot to address his followers. Others that he was a notorious highwayman who with his followers preyed upon the mule trains that passed that way. The 'chair' may have been a convenient look-out place, a common enough term found in a variety of forms. Lord Berkeley's Seat on An Teallach, the second finest mountain in Britain, would be such an example. Alternatively, as 'chair' is an obsolete term for pulpit, perhaps the religious explanation should hold sway.

Though the source of place-names is an interesting enough study, the next port of call, Windgather Rocks, will cause little debate. This popular and exposed gritstone outcrop was once the scene of a minor skirmish between landowner and climber. In an attempt to prevent access, it was barricaded with barbed wire, holds were chiselled off and pitch was applied to lower parts of the rocks. As Windgather, for gritstone, is unusually blessed with an abundance of holds, the efforts of the farmer merely made the routes more sporting and the fight was soon abandoned. Today it is usually busy with strings of learners who have forsaken the National Curriculum for more uplifting pursuits at the hands of their educational mentors.

My own beginnings had no such guiding hand. Phil and I had walked around most of the Lake District without particular difficulty, but a visit to the Stubai Alps made us realise that real mountains required a little more than stout hearts and a pacamac. We had also heard a rumour that even in the Lake District there lurked a summit that could only be reached by the use of ropes and other such paraphernalia. Neither of us knew anyone who climbed, nor even anyone who knew anyone who climbed, as opposed to walked, in the hills. We borrowed from the library a copy of *Teach Yourself Mountaineering*, one of the several attempts by the English Universities Press to educate the masses. It seemed that people learnt on outcrops but the only ones mentioned seemed to be a considerable distance from where we lived. Even this quasi-official information appeared a little dubious, for the only other instructional literature I could lay my hands on was a volume entitled *British Mountaineering* by Claude E Benson, awarded to one Jack Barltrop in 1919 for attendance and good conduct at S James Hadleigh Sunday School. This cast serious doubts on the merits of tackling 'Practice Climbs on Low Crags'. The author warns that, whereas the expert may benefit from such an encounter,

to the unlessoned schoolboy in the Academy of Moun-
taineering it may prove a not wholly unmixed bless-
ing. He is likely to come to erroneous conclusions.
Excellence as a rock-gymnast does not necessarily
constitute excellence as a rock-climber. Some day or
another, I fear me there will be a smash directly trace-
able to this ultra-gymnastic bouldering which is be-
coming increasingly the fashion. I only hope it will
require the services of the doctor and nurse, not of
coroner and sexton.

That might have been the end of that but Phil, during a local train journey, spotted what appeared to him to be a crag by the edge of a river. He had been allowed only a glimpse before it was lost to view and it had only attracted his attention because the low evening sun had seemed to reflect from its surface. In just such a way, it is reputed, was Craig yr Ysfa spotted from the summit of Scafell. With the aid of the Ordnance Survey and the town's Bus Timetable we tracked it down and in the latter part of a cold November afternoon set out to face our lot with the equally chilly words of Claude E Benson echoing in our ears:

I was going to say, 'I hope this note of warning is
needless,' but that would not be true, for I am con-

vinced that it is urgently necessary. I do hope, how-
ever, that my voice is the voice of Jonah, not of
Cassandra. It will be remembered that the people of
Nineveh mended their ways.

Between the two books there were a number of
sketches that purported to show what a rock climb
might look like; the one that stuck in my mind was
labelled 'Crack and Slab'. To our delight, we immediately discovered such a configuration and I despatched my companion to the crest of the crag to
lower a top-rope. This duly arrived and with the
newly fathomed Tarbuck knot, the *dernier cri* of rope
management, I stepped boldly off the ground. The
first objective was a ledge some thirty feet above, at
which the crack terminated. All went well until at
about half-way matters came to a stop. My right foot
was stuck in the crack, my left raised to waist level. A
photograph would have suggested I was about to step
up. A cine-camera would not. I made a few half-
hearted attempts to stand on a hold that I mistrusted
whilst, at the same time, leaving go of the one piece
of rock that seemed to keep me *in situ*. The attempts
descended in ever decreasing fractions of determination and I was about to inform my anchor man
that I was going down for a rest when I heard a voice.

Bird nestin, mister?

I looked down (something I had been avoiding till this point) to see a semicircle of small boys who had clearly been watching my antics with some expectation. The question was repeated and another of the upturned faces volunteered,

I wunna bother mister. Birds, it explained carefully, *dinna nest in November.*

I explained, equally carefully, that I was not bird-nesting. I was in fact rock climbing.

Why don't you get on with it mister? You could jump from there.

I was trying to explain that the intention was to climb up rather than be lowered down when, disappointed that little dramatic was likely to occur, they drifted away. I called 'above' that I was about to descend and try a different approach. But there was no reply and the rope remained resolutely taut. I wouldn't go up and I couldn't go down. I could not recall that either Benson or the EUP had anything to offer on this situation.

Resolution came in the form of my earliest interlocutor. By some means, known only to small boys, he had reached the ledge some ten feet above my head.

Shall I give you a pull-up mister?

There is only so much wicked pride can stand. With a general flailing of legs and clutching of hands, I hauled myself on to what turned out to be a fairly commodious platform. The small boy, mistaking this flurry of violence as a sign of imminent retribution, had understandably fled. Having collected my wits, I ignored the slab and scrabbled (scrambled would be too technical a term) up a gully composed of dilapidated sandstone cemented by rotting vegetation. The rope was dutifully reeled in by a mute and dishevelled blue anorak.

Despite Benson's warning against over-exuberance which has caused many a slip after the successful assault on the summit, we had little further trouble in securing terra firma. The street lights illuminated any pitfalls and the colliery railway lines which we had crossed with earlier trepidation had by now been closed for the weekend. At first, a consideration of the events suggested a blow to our vaulting ambition. But, after a couple of pints of Jonson's Best, matters were seen in a different light. We now realised the wisdom of the admirable Benson in his dismissal of low-lying crags and determined that our next objective would be, if not the Grepon, at least the summit of Pillar Rock.

Once Windgather has been passed, the path cuts through a corner of the Goyt Forest and regains the ridge, which is followed for a few hundred metres. At an obvious dip, a path is taken which drops to a minor road. Farmland is then crossed to the hamlet of Taxal. It is during this crossing that the connoisseur of stiles will have a field day. They come in all shapes and sizes and there is no doubt that there is a wealth of revelation and rewarding academic study awaiting the right enthusiast. As a starter, the correlation of stile-type to stone-type and the efficacy of the Kissing Gate immediately spring to mind. This, however, merely scratches the surface and further investigation belongs to a more scholarly tome than this. Suffice to mention a portcullis device which, when raised, allows a dog to pass from one side to the other. The day when the decrepit is reduced to this mode of passage is the day to look for alternative amusements.

Taxal is reached and there are a variety of ways to Horwich End and the White Horse. Perhaps the best is through the churchyard and down to the river. However, it is worth having a look around, for Taxal was much more of a place in its time. The church is old and was certainly in existence in 1287 when William de Dounes was recorded as Rector. There was also an inn, The Royal Oak (more recently The Chimes). This appears to have been a hub of activity. The salt road passed by, bear-baiting took place in the courtyard and the proximity of the church ensured that the traditional counterpoise between solemnity and good cheer was suitably maintained. Whatever choice is taken, Whaley Bridge offers public transport to Buxton or, if you have timed it right, directly back to Macclesfield. Another possibility is a wild night out in Manchester, always assuming you have remembered to pack your tuxedo.

This is a very unambitious walk and can become even less venturesome if a descent is made immediately into the Goyt valley and a low level route followed on the east or west side of the reservoirs. Such an option would be suitable for the seriously halt and lame, a late start on a winter's day or for those who alighted at the Cat and Fiddle at a more commodious hour and felt it wiser, in the event, to keep as close to sea level as possible.

Nevertheless, the route is a journey with a purpose, rather than walking round in circles. There is no doubt that a round has a charm of its own, particularly if you can see where you're going and where you have been. But I prefer starting at A with the necessity of arriving at B. Cape Wrath to Kinlochbervie is at the extreme end of this concept. The only way to get to your starting point is by ferry across the Kyle of Durness, followed by a rickety bus ride to the lighthouse. The bus timetable is constructed to avoid the regular naval bombardment of the surrounding countryside. If you let the bus return without you, there is no alternative: you are faced with a pathless journey and a couple of potentially dangerous river crossings before Sandwood Bay and relative safety is reached. What the attraction is, I'm not quite sure. The mystics, no doubt, would see it as a microcosm of the journey through life. A rather inflated claim. There have, however, been times at the end of a rain-sodden day when heaven can appear in the shape of a dry pair of socks.

Two
Little Big Walks

More matter with less art
(Hamlet)

Y ou see, I thought that's what you meant by the 'Art'. You had discovered the secret of Long Distance Walking without walking long distances. Bliss without blisters, if you see what I mean.

The words returned and I took the point. There was, after all, such a thing as The Trades Description Act. The criticism at the very least deserved consideration and, if possible, reparation. But often this produces problems of its own and, to save future attacks from an enthusiastic literalist, it might be best to have a clear idea of what we are talking about. A starting point might be an appraisal of what is meant by a Long Distance Walk. The capital letters appear to imply some sort of status, like British Broadcasting Corporation, and the fact that it is similarly abbreviated, in works more authoritative than this, might add weight to that theory. So, it can be assumed that walking twenty-five miles in no particular direction and then returning to the starting point is, albeit walking a long distance, not an LDW.

To reach this status there seem to be required three vital constituents: length, shape and a sense of outcome. Length can mean one of two things. A great distance in a single journey (the Derwent Watershed) or a far greater distance completed in a continuous succession of journeys (the Pennine Way). In reality, it is a question of it being sufficiently long to be an adequate challenge. Yet even this is relative. Ten miles of Scottish moorland is 'longer' than the same distance across the Sussex Downs.

The second requirement, shape, is usually topographical. A coast-to-coast walk is an obvious example, a mountain chain another. Often the shape determines the third element, a sense of outcome. You start at indisputable point A and finish with a sense of fulfilment at point B. The coast-to-coast is a good enough example but a better is the watershed walk which keeps to the high ground above a lake or reservoir. The start and finishing point is clearly at the outflow and the route is defined by the lie of the land. Not all, however famous, are so satisfactory. The Pennine Way falters in its apparent concept of striding aloft on the backbone of England. It could as well start at Macclesfield, or Matlock, as Edale and after Garrygill it throws in the towel and concedes the high ground in favour of Hadrian's Wall and Bellingham Forest. The Cheviot and Wainwright, with his offer of a free pint at Kirk Yetholm, try to save the day but in the end it is a somewhat downtrodden route, uncertain of its beginnings or its ends.

All this may or may not be interesting but it does little to resolve the complaint of my much put-upon friend. So, how *do* we do an LDW without resorting to wld? The answer – do it in stages – is simple enough but not necessarily equally straightforward. The problem is that the ambitions of the long distance walker and the short distance stroller rarely coincide. If your idea of a day's walk is ten miles of tractable terrain, then straying on to most LDWs would very soon find you in no-man's land. You could, of course, camp at this point but high on the agenda of most short distance walkers are the earlier mentioned four Bs. If luck is on your side, roads may cross at convenient moments. However, although being dropped off and picked up is a reasonable solution for the shorter courses, the ever-earlier starts and mist-ridden grid references will quickly try the patience of the most ardent supporter of a spouse's

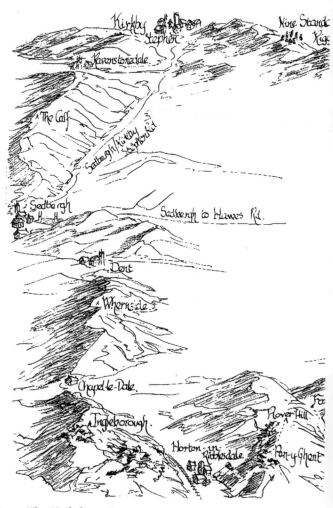

Route Two: The Yorkshire Centurion

Tan Hill Inn.

Langthwaite.

Grinton

Fremington

Castle Bolton

Aysgarth   Fors   River Ure

Northallerton to Hawes Rd.

Newbiggin.

× Naughtberry Hill

× Buckden Pike

Great Whernside.

R Wharfe

Arncliffe   Kettlewell.

G.R.Dale
Aug.'6

ambition. Of course, if you want to make a real fist of polluting what remains of the countryside, you could shuttle to and fro, abandoning cars at start and finish points. This plan tends to lose its edge when your only form of transport has been decommissioned by a herd of feral pit ponies or when you realise that in the more isolated sections you are spending as much time driving as walking.

But there is a solution whereby you can break the journey at a suitable juncture, sleep in a comfortable bed and drink as much as is reasonable without the fear of the breathalyser. Travel by train. Alight at station A, walk to station B, then take the return train home to your base. The next day, travel to B and walk to C, and so on. If the commuting becomes too arduous, you can move camp further up the line and continue the process. There may be no need to do this too often; a gentle locomotion in the morning can help the digestive system and after the conviviality of your evening stop, the return journey should pass quickly enough.

An obvious example of such a line is the Settle to Carlisle. This is seventy miles long and has ten stops. Admittedly, the last thirty miles look less interesting to the hill walker than the first forty. But the Settle to

Appleby section offers an interesting exercise in route planning and varied countryside. Carlisle could also be the starting point for a journey to Hexham via Hadrian's Wall. The Manchester to Sheffield line would facilitate a crossing of the Derbyshire Peak District. In Wales, both the Shrewsbury to Swansea and Llandudno to Dovey Junction (incorporating the Festiniog private railway) offer a myriad of stations only a few miles apart, all of which could be joined together by visits to the hinterland. There must be many others – there seem to be a number of branch lines in the West Country that may well be worth investigating – and more may come on the market as old lines are re-opened by local enthusiasts.

But there is no doubt which railway system in the British Isles bears the palm. ScotRail passes through some of the most dramatic scenery in Europe and my first trip will always be among the most vivid of mountain memories. I had caught the sleeper from Newcastle to Fort William, awakening with a call for breakfast somewhere around Crianlarich. By the time I had made my way to the dining car, the mist had started to lift and a wilderness unravelled before my eyes. Rannoch Moor, never seen but often visited in my childhood reading, seemed, as is rarely the case, more striking than previous imaginings. I had climbed and walked in most of the Lake District and Snowdonia but here the hills, the lochs, the rivers were on a different scale. The train took a perfect line, holding its height via bridges and viaducts, sidling through the protection of the fences and tunnels that for much of the year keep the snow at bay. Until, at last, it reached Corrour, a station in the middle of nowhere with no visible means of support. Never had coffee tasted so good. Nor such anticipation, since the day when I had persuaded my father that I was old enough to climb Helvellyn by Striding Edge.

So, if there is to be *the* train walk it has to be in Scotland and if what is wanted is a really Long Distance Walk, what better than a journey through the Highlands, starting outside Glasgow at Helensburgh and ending at Thurso? For via Fort William, Mallaig, Kyle of Lochalsh and Dingwall, if a boat is taken down the Sound of Sleat, there is a continuous train journey of 330 miles, punctuated by fifty-four stations. Of course, the gaps aren't equidistant. Some are close enough to be leapfrogged and others will force a day's journey of more than the stipulated ten miles, but all are within the compass of a reasonably strong walker who is prepared, when occasion demands, to put in a stint of seven to eight hours. The train timetables accommodate this need as, in general, there is a service first thing in the morning and a return early to mid evening. The exception to this is Sunday, when there are either no trains or inconvenient timings. Not that this is a bad thing. Medical study has shown that after six days of strenuous walking there is a danger of stress fractures to the feet if no rest is taken. You probably thought that the landed gentry were being benevolent in allowing the peasants a weekly day of rest. Far from it. In addition to a bit of brainwashing, courtesy of the local padre, its main concern was to get the work force up and running for Monday morning. As any schoolteacher knows, holidays are not a rest from labours past but a preparation for the task to come.

What appeals to me in this day of detailed route description is that you have to do the spade work yourself. Routes have to be planned and train times and overnight accommodation built into the schedule. In this the Ordnance Survey is the main source of information but another very useful publication is *Scottish Hill Tracks*, published by the Scottish Rights of Way Society. This describes in outline over three hundred cross-country paths and roads that follow ancient and traditional routes. Some of these are Coffin Roads which, as it turns out, are surprisingly long. The Macgregors of Glen Lyon buried their dead at the foot of Glen Orchy and when in 1830 Lady Mackenzie was laid to rest, it took five hundred men in turn to carry her the sixty miles from Gairloch to Beauly. But the majority of these tracks follow the line of old drove roads. They led from all corners to the regular markets or trysts where the Highlander traded his cattle with the English buyers. As the rearing and selling of cattle was the mainstay of the Highland economy, these roads form a complex network from Sutherland to the Borders and remain in existence thanks to the watchful eye of the Scottish Rights of Way Society.

The early efforts of this body were instrumental in raising public awareness of issues of access and rights of way. An awareness that was essential if pressure was to be brought to bear on all powerful landowners. In 1847 the Society funded the successful court action against the Duke of Atholl's attempt to close Glen Tilt as a public footpath, and forty years later a similar attempt to close Glen Doll failed in the face of the evidence that it had been long used as a drove road to take sheep from Braemar to Kirriemuir.

The landowner pursued the matter as far as the House of Lords, at a personal cost of £5000, and nearly bankrupted the Society in the process. But victory meant that landowners would in future be chary of risking the financial implications of contesting the right of walkers to use these ancient tracks for their own recreation.

Armed with relevant maps and the requisite time-tables, the walker can go as he pleases. He can take the shortest cut or meander into little visited glens and climb tops unconsidered by the compilers of Lists. There will be one or two stretches that will be longer than a short walk but a bit of thought can often sort it out. One such is the journey across Rannoch Moor from the Bridge of Orchy to Rannoch station. This is fifteen miles by rail across some pretty inhospitable country. There is a drove road which lands you at the west end of Loch Rannoch and five miles of road walking to the station. In fact, afforestation has destroyed the original line of the middle section and electrified fencing makes access problematic. It would be much better to bend the rules on this occasion and follow the West Highland Way to the Kingshouse. You could stay overnight (spare clothing can act as evening wear) and continue next day to Rannoch via Loch Laidon.

Because trains tend to go round mountains rather than over them, there are at times big loops which can be oxbowed by the determined walker. A classic example is the route through Glen Nevis from Corrour to Fort William, which is ten miles shorter than the rail journey. The direct route between Brora and Kildonan in the far north east is similarly productive. I am sure, on the other hand, there are some who would take an interest in visiting every station looking for their own particular Adlestrop. It is certainly worth noting that, in addition to the normal problems facing the walker in Scotland – river crossings, midges and high velocity rifles – there is also the little matter of *(x)* placed in the timetable next to the hour of arrival. This indicates a request stop and failure to inform the guard that you wish to alight will mean a somewhat longer distance walk than you planned.

For those averse to train-hopping, there is an alternative and that is a circular LDW. You are never too far from your starting place so your lines of supply are never unduly stretched. A good example and, in my opinion, the best of its type is the Yorkshire Centurion, a hundred-mile walk that circles the outer peaks of the Yorkshire Dales National Park. Devised by Jonathan Ginesi, it has 16,000 feet of climbing and covers every aspect of the countryside for which this area is renowned. What is more, there are sufficient stopping places for the route to be broken into sections to suit all needs. With a bit of organisation you could carry little more than a day sack.

The traditional starting point is Horton-in-Ribblesdale and the route follows the well-trod paths over Ingleborough and Whernside via the Hill Inn at Chapel-le-Dale. Paths and a bridleway lead to the distinctive cobbled streets of the village of Dent, where you follow the River Dee to Sedbergh. The route then traverses the Howgills, a set of miniature Lakeland fells, into Ravenstonedale and from there to Kirkby Stephen. The direction now swings east, ascending Nine Standards Rigg before crossing some tough country to Tan Hill. This inn at 1762 feet is the highest in England and provides a welcome haven if conditions have been extreme. It was built to serve the miners who during the week lived in bothies near the local workings, only returning to their homes at weekends. From here, just such a miners' track leads down to Whaw and Arkle Beck, which is followed to Langthwaite and Grinton. You are now over half-way and the character changes. The next objective is Aysgarth Falls.

This much visited tourist attraction is reached by climbing alongside Grinton Gill and traversing Greets Hill to Castle Bolton and thereafter to the Wheatsheaf Inn at Carperby. Paths then lead south to Aysgarth. Continue south through West Burton to Newbiggin and over Naughtberry Hill to the trig point of Buckden Pike. The next stop, via Great Whernside, is the village of Kettlewell. When I stayed there in 1979, the Bed & Breakfast proudly displayed the stuffed remains of 'the last eagle in England'. They have since reappeared in the Lake District, where they remain unmolested. However, if the fate of recently introduced red kites is anything to go by, they will probably stray south at their peril. The final stage cuts over the moor to Arncliffe, then takes in Foxup, Plover Hill and the last of the 'Three Peaks', Pen-y-ghent, the hill of the winds, before returning to your beginnings.

One of the charms of the walk is the villages and communities you pass through. If you had time to spare, you could break your journey to explore the way that humans have fitted into the landscape. Indeed, such a plan might encourage the previously mentioned domestic arrangements. One of the more interesting places is the market town of Sedbergh. There is much to visit and none more so, if you have an interest in mountaineering literature, than the Antiquarian Bookseller, R F G Hollett & Son in Finkle Street, which offers an excellent range.

Dominating the town is Sedbergh School, which has produced a number of outstanding athletes and sportsmen over the years. A major contributor to this reputation is a cross-country race of approximately ten gruelling miles. The race is held annually and is a red letter day in the school calendar. It started in 1881 as a paper-chase, until local farmers complained that the print on the paper was poisoning their sheep, whereupon it became an orthodox race around certain fixed points marked by poles. In 1913 The Ten Mile Steeplechase, as it was first known, was renamed The Wilson Run after its founder and long-serving housemaster, Bernard Wilson. He arrived at Sedbergh in 1876 and did much to help resuscitate a school practically at the point of extinction. He was a great believer in the value of school games and long distance running and it was his enthusiasm in persuading boys and members of staff to take part that made it the event it has become.

The Wilson Run is not the oldest of its type – Shrewsbury School recorded a similar steeplechase in 1819 – but it has the greatest tradition. The course, apart from reversing direction in 1882, is virtually unchanged, starting outside Lupton House in Back Lane and finishing just beyond Danson House on Loftus Hill. More importantly, it has only been cancelled three times in its history – in 1936 because of illness in the school, 1947 because of the Arctic type weather and in 2001 as the result of an outbreak of Foot and Mouth. The disappointment in 1947 was enormous; even *The Times* commented on the cancellation, and plans were made by six of the most likely contenders to run it unofficially but the Headmaster got wind of the scheme and the course was placed out of bounds.

The run's fame rested not only on its continuity but, particularly, on the race of 1899, the story of which is embedded in the folklore of the school and the town. C E Pumphrey, runner-up in the previous two years, beat his great rival W B Grandage by seven and a half seconds. The time of 1.10.16 was a record but not especially remarked upon. These were two very strong runners – both won Blues for cross-country – and their respective strengths no doubt drew each other on. Such was the competition at the time that it was generally assumed that the record would not be a fixture for long. But a fixture it became and nearly a century was to pass before it was eventually broken. W E H Long came within ten seconds in 1977 and he must have had high hopes that with another year at school he might be the one to lay the bogey. But either the conditions or the occasion got to him and it was not to be.

As the years passed the legend grew, helped by the Boys' Own image of Pumphrey himself. When at Cambridge, he also won a Blue for rugby and still found time to take a first in Classics. During the World War, he was twice mentioned in despatches and awarded the MC. In 1917 he lost an arm but in later life was still regarded as a superlative shot and a keen fisherman.

When the population of the town was at its height, interest in the race was considerable. A number of sweepstakes were run and sidebets made. Boys were solicited for information on form and the school barber was thought to have inside information. A former winner, Guy Waterworth, a Blackburn accountant, would arrive the day before the race and stay at the White Hart. He would sell as many half-crown stakes as he could, regardless of the number of runners, with a resultant handsome prize for the winner. Nor was the interest confined to the area. In the Thirties, the national newspapers covered the race and it was even filmed by Pathé, with nationwide distribution. Although the outcome was naturally the main concern, there was always one eye on the clock but no one could get near the record. Fifty years later, only five winners had completed the course in under seventy-five minutes – something that Pumphrey had done on three successive occasions. In the year of the Golden Jubilee doubts were cast. Had the course been shorter? Was timekeeping as accurate? Did the runners have the advantage of pacemakers? Naturally this produced a furore. However, after investigations had been completed it was generally held that the runners of the present day were faced with the same conditions as their predecessors and that an explanation lay elsewhere. The most popular theory was that the old school were essentially fitter and spent more of their time on the fells. As Pumphrey himself put it,

Compared with more recent years, we had the advantage of having to use our feet much more, year in and year out, than people do in these days of motoring.

But reading the accounts, I feel that much of the credit must go to the staff and particularly Wilson. There are many examples in school and youth sport where the inspiration of an individual or group of individuals can raise standards considerably above the norm and this can gather momentum as each year strives to outdo its predecessor. Eventually, this bubble bursts and the norm returns.

Nowadays, teachers faced with increasing risk of litigation and increasing workloads no longer feel able to contribute to the all-round development of the child. So it is left to the parent, often equally busy, to take over the task. Perhaps in these days of early retirement, grandparents could fill the breach. I could suggest a three-day expedition which not only introduces the child to wilderness country but also fits in with the general philosophy of this chapter. You take advantage of the fact that at one point the Scottish east and west coast train lines are forced to within twenty miles of each other. Leave the Inverness train at Dalwhinnie and follow the estate road along Loch Ericht to Ben Alder Lodge. Continue to Loch Pattock, then follow the Allt a Chaoil-réidhe to Culra Bothy (523762). This is the first port of call, which allows a relatively late start. Next day, follow the path over

Bealach Beithe and descend via one of Prince Charlie's many caves to Ben Alder Cottage (499680), which is the venue for the second bothy night. Depending on the age of the party, Beinn Bheoil, which gives a fine viewpoint, can be ascended en route. Ben Alder cottage is one of the best known bothies in the Highlands and the scene of many a Hogmanay celebration. It also supposedly has a ghost. There are reports of pacing footsteps and the sound of furniture being dragged across empty rooms. The truth is probably very big mice. The final day takes you west of Ben Alder itself over Bealach Chumhainn, then down to Corrour Station via Loch Ossian.

If you have time, don't rush back but stay a night at the Bridge of Orchy Hotel, where you can fully appreciate the virtues of a hot bath, clean clothes and a meal cooked by somebody else. I did all this many years ago with my son, then in his last year at primary school. For my benefit, we included an ascent of Beinn Eibhinn, an escaped Munro, and we each found the whole experience particularly rewarding. The distances are not great, which allows time for pottering, and you have elbow room if streams are in spate and detours have to be made. As with much of the Highlands, this is a deer forest and should be avoided when stalking is in place. As circumstances dictated the journey had to be made in August, I wrote to the estate explaining my plans. I received a courteous and helpful reply. Whenever I felt the circumstances merited, I have always requested permission. I have never been refused.

A final word of warning, keep your eye on the weather. Even in summer, the temperature can drop below freezing in this isolated upland area. In winter, as the events of December 1951 proved, possible death is never far away. Five experienced mountaineers left Corrour station to join some friends at Ben Alder Cottage. Long before they reached the Bealach Chumhainn, they decided to abandon the attempt and turn back to the safety of Corrour Lodge, a distance of no more than three miles. But they had now turned into the wind which had suddenly got up and was gusting to a hundred miles an hour. It took the one survivor seven hours to complete the journey. The other four were literally battered to death. The rescue party found the bodies of the four men within sight of safety. The survivor was a woman.

Three
An Easy Day For A Lady?

O tiger's heart wrapped in a woman's hide
(Henry VI Part 3)

On a sunny evening in August 1953 two men, 'Larry' Lamb and John Sumner, jogged down Matlock Bank and entered the approaches to the railway station with a turn of speed that took the reception committee rather by surprise. The two men had just completed what was to be regarded as the hardest continuous walk in the area, the Horseshoe of the Peak. The route followed the western gritstone edges, starting at the Roaches in Staffordshire, and after crossing the moorland peatbogs of Kinder, Bleaklow and Featherbed Moss, picked up the eastern edges of Stanage, Burbage, Froggatt *et al*, to reach its eventual destination via the parklands of Chatsworth House. The journey exceeded sixty miles and, for the most part, the weather had been atrocious.

It is possible to walk further, and I am sure many have done so, but there was a certain logic in the nature of the chosen route. In a sense it is the coping stone placed on the framework of local long distance walking that has its 1880s foundations in the Manchester YMCA Rambling Club and is supported by such pillars as Cecil Dawson and Fred Heardman. In the first place, it completely covers the ground, marching the rough bounds of the White Peak, the area's limestone core. Second, it accurately reflects the terrain of the Dark Peak. On one hand, pleasant walking along the tops of the grey gritstone edges with easy going and fine perspectives. On the other, desolate moorland where, in bad weather, it's often one step back for each two forward and the view is little more than the edge of the grough you find yourself traversing or the mud-spattered gaiters of the man in front. Perhaps this is what attracts people to the area – this oxymoron of free-limbed exhilaration and unrelenting and often unrewarding toil.

But this was half a century ago and Lamb's time of twenty-eight hours must seem a dawdle to those who nowadays trot round the forty miles of Derwent Watershed in under five. No doubt, it has suffered the same fate as the great Alpine courses that challenged our Victorian forebears. These were first described as Inaccessible, with added warnings of ogres and man-eating eagles. Then, through a bombardment of ropes, ladders, metal attachments and, for all I know, strategically placed pieces of dynamite, they tumbled down the enumerated scales of Difficulty until they glissaded, at last, into the appellative disgrace of 'An Easy Day for a Lady'.

So, who were these ladies who were only allowed out when the going was deemed sufficiently soft? There was no evidence that they formed part of the support team that 'whipped in' Lamb and Sumner in their attempt on the Last Great Peak District Challenge. If they were part of the reception committee, it was probably to proffer the thermos and sigh admiringly. If this was not the case, it was an exception that must have tested the general rule. When females at that time took part in male-dominated sports, and thus by definition any sports of serious note, it was on the domestic side, making cream teas and selling raffle tickets to finance further brave ventures of athleticism. When their job was done, they shuffled off to feed the babies and polish the furniture.

But, at face value, climbing should be less sexist. When men and women climb together, they are equally in each other's hands. They can both end up equally dead. Yet anyone who has been a member of a climbing club can see there are hidden agendas.

Men can peacock around and women realise the possibilities of exclusive access to the object of their desire. However, the intimacy of cramped stances and sheltering boulders may appear alluring but can quickly fade. Too often, familiarity reduces the moment of shared contact to the increasingly exasperated, *You can't possibly be tired. We've only just started.* Or, *How can you expect me to remember where every single hold is? It seemed perfectly obvious to me.* It is usually at this point that the attractions of Action Man start to recede in favour of the five-star alternatives on offer, while men realise that if they want to achieve their objectives, they are better off sticking to their own kind. Certainly, it soon became apparent to women that if they also wanted to be serious climbers and have their climbing taken seriously, they would have to do likewise and it was against this background that the Pinnacle Club was formed.

The club was founded in 1921 in Manchester and was seen by some as an extension of the women's movement of the 1880s. It was championed by the *Manchester Guardian* and attracted support from those who wished to avoid male-orientated societies or were denied access to male-exclusive clubs. One of the problems that faced Pat Kelly and her fellow found-

ing members was that women would join not necessarily to climb but rather to demonstrate solidarity
with the female cause. This, of course, was not the
fundamental point of the venture, so it became necessary to introduce a rule whereby it was only possible to become a full member if you could lead climbs
at a certain standard and showed a commitment to
teaching other women to reach a similar level. Inter-
estingly, it was the only climbing club in the country
that had such a restriction to membership.

The name also caused problems. All agreed it was
not going to be called The Ladies Climbing Club
but there were those that wanted the word 'Women'
to appear in the title and those that thought the term
'Pinnacle' was offering too obvious a hostage to fortune. The latter may well have been right. There were
any number of men who were willing to patronise
and women who were quick to disapprove. Dorothy
Pilley recalls 'hard stares from the women and snig-
gers from the louts' when she appeared in Coniston
dressed in trousers and climbing boots. It is difficult
now to realise the problems that women climbers
faced before they got anywhere near the rock face.
The history of the club tells of women deceptively
dressing for church before changing behind stone

walls into more appropriate garb for the Sunday meet. In one case, a member went to extreme lengths to escape parental disapproval. To avoid the discovery that she had spent her vacation mountain-climbing, she used to pre-write a series of holiday postcards. She then arranged for them to be despatched from the various seaside resorts that she was supposedly visiting. Even in the 1960s my now wife had difficulty convincing her mother that the bruises on her knee were caused by being jammed in a crack half-way up Scafell Crag, rather than the result of other and more dubious pursuits. In many ways, the situation is summed up by the story of a Pinnacle member, Alex White, leading a fellow member up Eve, a VS, on Shepherd's Crag. The climb was busy and she was waiting in a queue at the foot of the second pitch. When the preceding party were well ahead she started to climb, only to be hailed from below by a concerned male voice: *I should wait a little while, dear, your leader hasn't reached the stance.* As this was 1981, the riposte must have been quite interesting.

The problems that some early members had fore-seen surfaced in an article in *Mountain* written by Ian McNaught-Davies. The writer had become through his appearances on television the authoritative voice on British Rock Climbing, organising several TV spectaculars on Cloggy and elsewhere. For the most part, he was irreverent and satirical and the article in question was no exception. It took a general swipe at single-sex groups, with particular reference to the members of the Pinnacle Club. The account was not flattering. To make matters worse, he had already accepted an invitation to speak at the club's Annual Dinner. He protested that he was trying to do women's climbing a service; the serious part of his argument was that by isolating themselves they were in fact accepting that they were second best. However, his protestations were in vain and a carefully worded meet report showed that, like their illustrious precursor, who also tramped the high lands of Britain, the members were not amused.

As with all satire, particularly when it causes offence, there was probably some truth in his remarks. Even a casual reading of the history of the club shows a different picture from that of the average male-dominated organisation. There is much talk of pastries and trifles, marriage and babies, the highlight of a meet at Castle Naze when Pat Kelly turned up with a basket of strawberries, members floating back to the hut in an intoxicated haze after a half pint of shandy *each*. Their attitude to the furnishings of the club hut at Cwm Dyli ('Heaven for a bob a day') is more domestic than its male equivalent. There was certainly a difference. Whether that made it better or worse depends on what you think the whole thing is all about.

However, if the aim is to be the best, you must compete with the best. There is no point in moaning about glass ceilings if you are prepared to lounge on the withdrawing room floor. Unlike most activities invented by men, climbing is relatively easy for women to access. Whether you are prepared to lead Central Buttress, Great Slab, Cenotaph Corner, XYZ Super Direct or whatever is the test piece of the age doesn't depend on your sex but on your attitude and your ability. I do not mean to give the impression that it was all cakes and ale at the Pinnacle Club. Many triumphs are also recorded in the same account, from the minor when Shirley Bull's *Scrambling Guide to the Cuillin* was published by that most male of bastions, the Scottish Mountaineering Club, to the major climbing successes of the Club in the Alps and Himalayas. What is more, its membership included the authors of two of the best books written about mountaineering: *Climbing Days* by Dorothy Pilley and

Space Below My Feet by Gwen Moffat.

This last remark is, I suppose, a rather sweeping statement and I ought to do my best to justify it. To start with, both books seem to have an air of intellectual honesty which is often lacking in the writings of their male contemporaries. When men put pen to paper, the combination of not wanting to lose face on one hand, yet appear modest on the other, often seems to constrict or stifle a genuine response. There were exceptions. Menlove Edwards, whose writing in many ways bridges the worlds of the two women, was one. But Edwards, a homosexual and a pacifist in time of war, was as much an outsider as they were. Indeed, there is an argument that all the best writers look in from the outside. When you are swimming with the crowd, you can't see much for the spray. Another piece of evidence is that they make the cut and if women do that they are probably better than their male equivalent. Not many do. In *The Winding Trail* and its fellow anthology *Mirrors in the Cliffs*, an otherwise balanced collection of writing on walking and climbing, of the two hundred or so extracts only five percent are from female contributors. The fact that both Pilley and Moffat have the accolade of a Neate star and elbowed their way into a mountaineering canon dominated by the ghosts of Whymper and the Abraham Brothers must be an indication of something.

Regardless of their literary impact, they both made a considerable splash with their fellow members. Pilley, after Pat Kelly's unfortunate death, became the doyenne of the Club. It is easy to see the reasons for the reverence in which she was held. As a writer – her first cheque bought her own climbing rope (Beale's with the red strand) – she symbolised the social and financial independence that lay behind the general philosophy of the women's movement. As a mountaineer – her range of experience both at home and abroad was more than a match for most men – she showed that women could compete as equals. Perhaps what was admired most was the manner in which she broke the ice. She climbed of her own accord. She had not been the dutiful female dragged along by others. In fact she admits, in *Climbing Days*, that when she started she didn't know any climbers, whether family, friends or in the workplace. It was, as she said, not like tennis: 'In those days *everybody* played tennis.' Also, in terms of social behaviour she would flout tradition. There is a story of how she refused to be bullied by the manageress of the Sligachan Hotel who insisted she wore a skirt when on the premises, even offering to lend her an appropriate garment. Pilley's unambiguous response was to go down to dinner in trousers, disdaining that 'full, black emblem of respectability'.

But it was, perhaps, because she saw the point of the Pinnacle Club that she was most approved. It was not founded as a feminist gesture. It offered the opportunity for women to understand the full responsibility of leadership. Something they could never achieve unless they climbed without men. She supported the idea of qualification as it ensured that all members of the party were part of a competent entity and not just being tagged along like so many sheep. She also argued that in many types of climbing, women could be the equal of men. Indeed, with their lower centre of gravity, their balance might be naturally superior. She conceded sheer muscular power, but points out that it is not the force available but how it is used that counts. Nor was this theory alone. She would spend hours encouraging others, often sacrificing her own climbing opportunities. Her writings never stinted praise nor showed the slightest sign of envy in reporting the success of her fellow members. Her tribute to Pat Kelly after her fatal accident is both elegant in its construction and moving in its content.

Despite all this, she was still restricted by the mores of her times; most of her big climbs were with her husband and his male friends. It would take a World War to change that. The Club News Sheet of 1940 tells of members serving in the WRNS and ATS, driving ambulances and contributing to all branches of the medical service. Having been given the responsibility by default, some were unlikely to surrender it gracefully and there must have been a feeling, in certain quarters, of what we have we hold.

One such woman was our second author, Gwen Moffat. Unlike Dorothy Pilley, climbing was not the initial liberating experience. She left the Land Army and enlisted with the ATS during the war in order to get near to what she thought was the action. She found the restrictions irksome, and deserted. On the run, she lived with a group of conscientious objectors, sharing cheap accommodation in remote hill cottages, surviving on casual labour and often sleeping rough. Eventually she realised that her life had no shape, so surrendered to the authorities and finished her time. But the experience left two marks: a love of mountains and a desire for independence.

Her autobiography tells of the problems of the single woman. Living by herself and relying on the generosity of others for transport, she was always liable to be sexually harassed, on one occasion waking to find a supposed pillar of society in her bedroom and in another particularly violent and frightening episode being dumped in a remote lay-by in the middle of France. Like Pilley, she hoped to make an independent living through writing but, as things turned out, it was the mountains and her skill at rock climbing that offered early financial stability. Moffat quickly realised that she was as good, if not better, a climber as most men and decided to become a professional guide with the appropriate BMC certification. All this was complicated by the fact that she was, in effect, a single mother and had to rely on others to look after her daughter while she looked after her clients.

It was during this period of her life that she applied to join the Pinnacle Club. She attended a meet on Lliwedd so she could demonstrate the necessary skills to qualify. It was summer and, as usual, she was climbing in bare feet. She was also pregnant; in fact the baby was due any time. Much panic amongst the members and much debate as to the safest way to get her off the crag. Moffat resolved the matter by declaring that, as speed seemed to be of the essence, it would be best if she led the shortest, albeit the hardest, variation to the summit.

The Pinnacle Club proved a refuge in more ways than one. The members encouraged mother and daughter to move into the club hut and with that 'minor anxiety' removed, Moffat was able to plan ahead. Her only alternative bolt hole had been with her mother in Sussex and that was not where she really wanted to be. The plan seemed to have worked for the book ends on an upbeat, with a sense of fulfilment. Jack Longland in his Foreword describes *Space Below My Feet* as 'a remarkable book by a remarkable woman' and there is no doubt she was. There are men who have lived as rough, Orwell, for example, in the spikes of London and the slums of Paris. But for her it was different. As she recalled at one of her lowest moments,

Poverty without responsibility is amusing and unconventional, but to a woman with a family it is squalor.

Perhaps the example of combined co-operation and independent sense of purpose that seems to reflect the general tone of the Pinnacle Club can suggest a

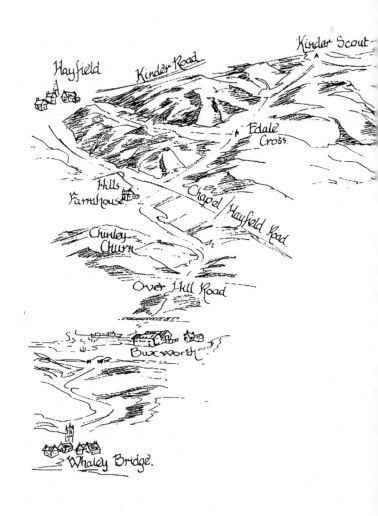

Route Three: The 'Wayfarer's' Peak Horseshoe

Edale

Train to Edale.

Grindleford

Froggatt Edge.

Froggatt

Curbar Edge

Curbar

Baslow Edge

GR Dale.   Aug '02

Baslow.

solution to one of the problems of the twenty-first century: the provision of adequate public transport in remote areas of the countryside. In the 1950s Kay Boucher reported that she and her friends became part of the Travelling Climbers Grapevine. The law at the time did not allow private coaches to advertise their destination and time of departure. This was to avoid competition with public transport. But coaches were hired and the grapevine operated. Climbers mysteriously appeared with the appropriate gear, to be swept along the A5 to camp in the farm below Tryfan and spend the weekend on the cliffs of the Ogwen Valley. In a similar way, but for different reasons, there are today bands of enthusiasts who are trying to reconstruct a transport system. These are rail enthusiasts replacing the track and rolling stock destroyed by the Beeching axe. One such line is that from Matlock to Buxton, which has so far reached Rowsley. If, perhaps with public money, they could be assisted to complete the journey, this would be a very welcome addition to the walking in the district, opening up access to the limestone dales and offering a mix-and-match option for a day in the Dark and White Peak.

Perhaps there is also a general principle to be investigated. I don't know but I guess that the major saving the Government effected by closing branch lines was in wages rather than the cost of sleepers or the price of diesel fuel. A lot of people retire early these days and remain in active working health for longer. Perhaps such people, or at least those who were denied a train set in their youth, would volunteer to re-open and staff such a system, particularly at weekends. After all, they have the rest of the week to follow their own pursuits. A complete rail network is the backbone of an effective transport plan, moving people by day and goods by night. It is clear to everyone that longer life is going to put a considerable strain on the economy and the social infrastructure. Maybe National Service for the over-sixties is part of the answer. Certain ladies, if asked, might agree that being given an opportunity to do your bit produced a sea change in the past.

Four
Catabasis

Letting 'I dare not' wait upon 'I would'
Like the poor cat i' the adage.
(Macbeth)

The Cat and Fiddle may not be quite the highest inn in England but it has the most commanding position. A drop of water falling at this point has an equal chance of arriving in either the Mersey or the Trent and so into the two seas that wash the shores of Britain. It was built by John Ryle, a Macclesfield banker, in about 1830 and was much appreciated by travellers on the new turnpike between Macclesfield and Buxton. The origins of its name are uncertain. One suggestion is that it was named after Catherine le Fidele, wife of Czar Peter the Great. A more likely explanation is that it was named after the popular game of trap ball where a small stick (cat) was placed in a baking dish (trap) in such a way that when struck by a larger stick (fiddle) it sprang in the air, to be hit again, one assumes, as far as possible. A game that clearly required excellent hand-eye co-ordination and seems to have degenerated into a pastime that is both more exclusive and expensive.

You are at the Cat and Fiddle, so what's the best way back to Macc? The simplest route and in some ways the most satisfying, as there is a sense of continuous progress towards your objective, is via Wildboarclough, Shutlingsloe, Macclesfield Forest and the Langley reservoirs. The route follows a broad moorland track in a southerly direction. After half a mile or so, leave it for a path that leads (at times all too literally) into Cumberland Brook. This path in turn joins a track which, passing above a pleasant wooded gorge, finally drops into the valley at Clough House. The footpath through the farmyard picks up the right of way that connects Wildboarclough and Langley. There was a time when Shutlingsloe was the forbidden mountain and trespassers were made to feel particularly unwelcome. But this now well established path leads across the moor, skirting the summit to the north. However, the opportunity to reach the top should not be missed, as the hill is so sufficiently separate that it offers excellent views in all directions and particularly to the south and west. In fact, with the aid of the summit viewfinder and map, you could sit and plan most of the routes in the immediate area.

The descent and trek across the rather damp moor

are greatly facilitated by large slabs of stone which form a staircase and track to the drained walks of the Forest. Some of these slabs originated from a burial ground in Macclesfield and were transported by helicopter to their present site. Although they have been respectfully sand-blasted, remnants of inscription can still be seen. (Whether this is the rocky road envisaged by the prisoner of Bedford Gaol is hard to say, but at least progress of some sort can be assumed now that we have learnt to climb on the shoulders of our ancestors.) Whatever your views on this conversion, at least the modern-day pietist will be relieved to learn that the space freed up by the removal of the stones is now the unsullied and respectable resting place of the motor car whenever its owner goes shopping.

Macclesfield Forest is reached and the steep walks are descended in the direction of Trentabank Reservoir, where a road can be joined which takes you to Langley. It is, however, considerably better to follow the signs for the Gritstone Trail, which takes you along the south side of Ridgegate Reservoir. When you are clear of the trees, there is a surprise view across the water and the discerning will pick out the weathered stonework of the Leathers Smithy which, if you have timed it right, offers an excellent opportunity for lunch.

Rejoin or continue along the Gritstone Trail past Bottoms Reservoir until it (the trail, not the reservoir) starts to ascend Teggs Nose. Leave it at this point and enter the village along the attractive pond-lined Holehouse Lane. Walk through the village until, shortly after Langley Hall, field paths lead to the Hollins and the boundaries of Macclesfield Golf Course.

As a general rule, I am of the American humorist's persuasion that golf is a good walk spoiled. I also wonder why a group of selected individuals should have the right to fence off large tracts of walkable countryside and claim its exclusive use for what appears a pastoral version of Hunt the Thimble. No doubt, they will claim that they have as much right to recreation as the next man but a train journey from Macclesfield to Manchester is telling. Before reaching Stockport, the train passes through acres of carefully manicured fairways occupied, for the most part, by a few middle-aged and, no doubt, middle-class males. (I say males, as women appear to play an inferior part in the proceedings, being corralled into separate quarters and only allowed out at regulated intervals. No doubt they are made suitably aware that one of the indictments which led to the demise of Mary Queen of Scots was that she had the temerity to play golf.) But once Stockport is passed, there seems to be little to encourage athletic activity unless one counts a few square yards of astroturf that signifies the efforts, I expect against the odds, of Manchester Eagles Junior Football Club. No wonder the talk at the nineteenth centres around the irresponsible nature of the current younger generation. Of course, the golf club is not the only, let alone last, bastion of those values that made the Empire great. But I imagine it would be jolly pleased if it were.

Despite these misgivings, I was quite taken by an account of a former Club Captain. He seems to have adopted a more primal approach and decided to drive a golf ball from the first tee of the Macclesfield Club to the Cat and Fiddle. I was taken, in the sense that he seems to be respecting the essential nature of the game. Golf or, to give it its correct nomenclature, *kolf,* was invented by the Dutch. Whilst waiting for the canals to freeze, which would allow the more invigorating pastime of ice-skating, they were in the habit of striking an egg-shaped ball from windmill to windmill in the least number of blows possible. The game was refined by the Scots who, in the absence of windmills, knocked stones into rabbit holes with the crooks of their upturned walking sticks. The English, whose sole contribution to the *genre* was the game of Pall Mall, a more violent form of croquet, attacked the problem with their practised colonial zeal and managed to surround the game with their usual hugger-mugger and delight in legal niceties. So, it was refreshing to hear that earlier traditions had not been completely lost and I followed the detail with unusual interest.

The course was divided into twenty-one 'holes' across ten separate parcels of farmland. The pursuit was completed in a shade under five hours, with a suitable pause at the Stanley Arms. The technical details, for those who understand such matters, are – clubs used: 3 wood x 43, 7 iron x 14, wedge x 5; total strokes: 62; lost balls: 3; total, including one stroke per lost ball: 65. The match report suggested that the last three holes were very difficult, various large wagons being part of the natural hazards. The gentleman in question is also to be congratulated on arranging the course so that it avoided the various pedestrian rights of way that cross the area.

As we continue along the edges of the golf course,

there are a number of fine viewpoints. From this elevation you can see Macclesfield as the town it once was. Despite the best efforts of town planners, church spires and towers still catch the eye and the worse commercially-driven blemishes are hidden from sight. Soon the outskirts are reached and the streets falling into the town quickly reach the canal. Turning right on to the towpath, the walk concludes most felicitously at the Puss in Boots, where the appropriate debriefing can take place. You are now back on the A537 and a stroll down the hill brings you to the railway and bus stations.

The journey also takes me back. As a child I knew the area, not from personal contact, but through maternal folklore. I remember one particular story about my great-grandmother, a young lady who clearly had a greater affection for the town than for her rural existence. She was taken to Macclesfield once a fortnight and, whilst her father attended the fatstock market, she purchased her haberdashery and, no doubt, laid her plans. On her return, she would sit at the back of the trap, clutching her ribbons, staring steadfastly in the direction of the retreating lights, until, at some point, the land rose to conceal them and they finally disappeared from view. But she had her wish, entangled a silkmaster and lived in a house newly built in the centre of the town. Alas, events did not end happily, with the advent of artificial silk and the demise of her husband, who was struck on the head by a cricket ball propelled from the neighbouring Grammar School. This, now, all sounds rather Barbara Cartland but as a child the story touched me and, I suppose, with sufficient deftness, if I feel the imprint still.

* * * *

If this walk seems rather pusillanimous, the journey can be extended by two convolutions. Both ignore the turning to Cumberland Brook and continue to the A54. Descend past a ventilation shaft that serviced Dane Colliery and follow the river, or take a higher and drier route through the quarries to Three Shires Head. This is the junction of four packhorse ways leading into Cheshire, Staffordshire and Derbyshire and the trains of up to fifty animals, bells ringing to warn of their arrival, must have welcomed the refreshment of the Panniers Pool.

The packhorse was traditionally the only way of transporting goods in bulk and, as the rough moorlands did not favour horse-drawn wagons, the practice continued in the Peak District into the nineteenth century. Generally, the Galloway pony was the favourite breed, but in this part of the world the German Jaeger seemed to be more popular. The fact that the single man who led the train was known as the 'jagger' would support this claim, as would the place names such as Jaggers Gate and Jaggers Clough. The merchandise was carried in two panniers fixed to a saddle, capacious enough to carry two and a half hundredweight of coal. Nor were the packhorses as slow a method of transport as you might imagine. Records show that salmon were carried from Workington in Cumbria to London, where they were sold 'fresh' at a handsome profit. Clearly there must have been a very well organised relay system to allow such a possibility. One of the early carriers in the area was Thomas Pickford of Poynton and it would be a pleasing coincidence if he were related to James Pickford, also from Cheshire, who founded the renowned transport company a century after.

One of these ways is a track which leads back to the A54. When you reach Cut-thorn, cross fields and the main road. Paths and quiet lanes continue into Wildboarclough. The second and longer way crosses the bridge at Three Shires Head and takes a track that skirts Turn Edge. At the apex, paths lead down fields to the road between Allgreave and Flash. Take the track to Manor Farm and pass through it to reach the Youth Hostel at Gradbach.

The Hostel was originally a mill built by Thomas Dakeyne and, although the waterwheel has gone, you can judge its unusual size by the dimensions of its housing. It was first used to spin flax, then waste-silk until eventually, in conjunction with a mill in Wildboarclough, it produced carpets. The route that you are about to follow is the packhorse way that carried the necessary material from one to the other.

This is typically narrow. As the pony's uncloven hooves would quickly sink in mud, the ways had to be roughly paved and the local parishes found it cheaper and easier if the width was restricted to a couple of feet. Hence the warning bells attached to the harness, as in many places it was impossible for two trains to pass. At the top of the climb, the jagger could have called at the Eagle and Child to allay potential dehydration. The building is still there but is no longer a pub, though the badge of the Stanley family, emblazoned with raptor and infant, is still to be seen above the door. The Stanleys made a judicious decision at the battle of Bosworth and were rewarded for their acumen by elevation to the Lordship of Derby. As a result, there is much evidence of their presence in the area. The Bate Hall, the oldest inn in Macclesfield, was originally their town house and before the shopping mall had its way there was both a Derby and Stanley Street. The town even boasted a further Eagle and Child. Our way continues, at times deteriorating into a footpath, and passes the farm at Tagsclough before entering Wildboarclough.

This route may have carried carpets but by far the most important merchandise in the area was salt. This was an essential commodity for the preservation of meat and as such had great value. Its worth can be gauged by the cost of tolls on the turnpikes, where the charge for salt was fourteen times greater than for most other goods. The salt itself came from the brine pits of Cheshire at Northwich, Middlewich and Nantwich. These 'wiches' (the word originally meant dwellings) sent forth a steady stream of Salters who would transport the product across the Peak District to the various centres of population. They would, of course, use the same ways as the other packhorses but each Salter would have his own route. This became known as a saltway, and the placenames – Saltersford, Saltersgate, etc – reflect this. If you have examined a map of the former boundaries of Cheshire, you may have wondered why the county claimed a panhandle of land that drove a wedge between Lancashire and Derbyshire. The answer is that the first Earls of Chester, anxious to ensure safe passage of their valuable asset, claimed the way up Longdendale to Salters Brook and thus to the Yorkshire border.

There is one other form of ancient thoroughfare in the area and that is the English drove road. Although there are examples nearby, they skirt around this particular moorland area. To follow the packhorse routes would be too onerous, and resting and feeding places for both men and beasts too far apart. Unlike the packhorses the oxen, to ensure prime condition at the point of sale, would be driven no more than a dozen miles a day; pigs at half that rate. The pigs even wore woollen socks with leather soles to protect their feet.

The increase in use of these roads corresponded with the growth of city life. Conurbations unable to sustain themselves from the neighbouring countryside required herds of cattle being driven mainly from Wales, Scotland and Yorkshire to a series of Fairs or Markets. The expansion of the Navy also required

Macclesfield / Buxton Rd.

Puss in Boots.

Macclesfield Canal.

Golf Course.

Hollins.

Langley Hall

Bottoms Resr.

Heathers Smithys

Shutlingsloe

Wildboarclough

Eagle & Child

Route Four: Cat to Cat

Cat & Fiddle.

Three
Shires
Head.

R. Dane

Manor
Farm.

Gradbach

G. R. Dale
May '02.

enormous stocks of salted meat to be available in bulk. Although the main drove roads were elsewhere, there is an important exception close at hand. Part of the route from Cheshire to Nottingham and its famous Goose Fair was along 'The Great Road from Congleton to Winster'. This runs over Gun Hill and past the Mermaid Inn, eventually to cross the Dove at Hartington and join the well-established north-south drover's road at Wirksworth. It has been recorded that as many as 20,000 geese at a time were taken along this way to Nottingham. Their protective footwear was less sartorially elegant than that of the pigs and was applied by their being forcibly driven through a mixture of tar, sand and sawdust.

The drover was very much a cut above the average jagger. An Elizabethan Act of Parliament decreed that he must be at least thirty years of age and a married householder. In addition, he had to apply for a yearly licence signed by three Justices of the Peace. This suggested that he was a man to be trusted and, as such, he acted as a carrier, first of messages, then of money. In fact he became the first travelling bank. A merchant wishing to settle an account in a neighbouring town would pay the drover. Rather than risk carrying the money on the journey, the drover would leave it at home and pay the bill out of the sale of the cattle. In 1799 a Welsh drover, David Jones, founded the Black Ox Bank at Llandovery and issued notes engraved with the animal in question. The success of this venture can be measured by its continuance into the twentieth century and it only disappeared when it was eventually taken over by Lloyds.

Whatever connection John Ryle and the Cat might have had with this fiscal fraternity, our banker, if the longer routes have been taken, is the Crag Inn. This would be a suitable place for lunch and the post-prandial path to Shutlingsloe rejoins the main route. As to the technical detail – a novice length of string would judge the distances to be 13k, 16k, and 20k respectively. The experienced walker will, I'm sure, know better.

Five

An Insular Response

The isle is full of noises
Sounds and sweet airs, that give delight and hurt not.
(The Tempest)

There is no doubt that the number of people who aspire at any one time to collect the 3000-foot mountains of Scotland has most certainly risen in a dramatic fashion. What is more significant is the number who at any one time have actually completed the list of Sir Hugh T Munro. In the first quarter of the last century there were two. By the second, a further thirteen. In 1975 there were, according to the Keeper of the List at the Scottish Mountaineering Club, still only 132 who gloried in the title of Completionists, but by the millennium this number had also passed 2000. The early records were no doubt accurate. It was extremely unlikely that someone could go to the time and trouble of completing the round and be unknown to the climbing fraternity. Now anyone with sufficient leisure and a reliable motor car can set aside a decade or so to give it a go. Numerical accuracy must decline. While many, if not most, will dutifully report their doings to the appropriate authority, there will be others who, either through diffidence or sloth, will not. Indeed, the SMC may feel that the time has come to call it a day rather than ennoble the exploits of every Jack the Lad from south of the border.

Perhaps it was against this background that a group of individuals decided to call the inaugural meeting of The Munro Society in April 2002. This was to be an inclusive club, membership to be restricted to those who have achieved the target of ascending all the peaks – or what were considered all the peaks at the time of ascension. The aims of the society and the benefits of membership are explained at www.munrosociety.org.uk. The first were condensed into the idea that the group can 'give something back to the mountains'; the second that you could contact a significant number of fellow Munroists (as opposed to a number of significant Munroists) and indulge in various social gatherings. All this seems rather woolly. The only way you can give anything back to the mountains is by actively discouraging people from visiting them. The social activity advertised for the first meeting in Dundee was a buffet and quiz. I was not convinced that the promise of cucumber sandwiches and the opportunity to recall the spot height of Ben Sodhall would breathe life and fire into any enterprise. But as two hundred people turned up it must serve some need.

Perhaps, after the champagne bubbles have subsided, the Final Trig Point causes more problems than it solves. Yes, you have done it, but what have you actually done? As with much of life, the journey is often the thing. Once you have arrived, the goal can seem less satisfactory than was hoped. The problem is what to do next. The Corbetts or Grahams seem more of the same, the Bridges, Nuttalls or whatever something of an anti-climax. The Marilyns are a possibility but, with the isolated outposts of Stac Lee and Stac an Armin, they are a very different kettle from the not so inaccessible points of the Cuillin, and there are an awful lot of them. Perhaps, in retrospect, there is also a sense of disappointment with the event itself. In the end it is only a question of opportunity and money, coupled with a determination to place one foot in front of the other several thousand times, plus a bit of airy scrambling on the most adhesive rock in the country. As far as technical achievement is concerned, you might just as well have plodded up a nearby hill on the requisite number of occasions and taken in a weekend rock climbing course with the local Venture Scouts.

Perhaps there is a need to find out why anyone does it in the first place. What was it that caught the imagination? What compensation is on offer for the midges, driving rain and porridge-like snow? Or trudging up those hills that were nothing to look at and offered less when looked from? Of course, there are the good days, when you climb out of the cloud and spend a sun-blessed day traversing the mist-girt valleys, when a layer of frozen snow turns the travails of a bog-tussocked moorland into a stroll in the park. And there are a number of fine mountains with airy ridges and stupendous views. But these luxuries are not the preserve of the Munroist; in fact, the law of averages suggests that he will have more of the former horrors than the latter delights. The attraction, therefore, must lie elsewhere, perhaps in the act of collection itself, the realised ambition of having them all, from Ben Lomond to Ben Hope, neatly rounded up, ticked off, underlined in red, pinpointed on maps and, if that is your inclination, finally logged in the deepest vaults of the World Wide Web.

And as collections go, Munro-bagging has a lot in its favour. The number is about right to make it a challenge rather than an obsession. You finish with a good sense of the geography of the northern highlands of Britain. With the odd exception (the hills above Loch Rannoch spring to mind) it is obvious when you have achieved your objective and the SMC has thoughtfully provided a slim volume in which to record your efforts. But I suspect it is the idea of the completed bag that really appeals. Momentum is maintained by the inexorable countdown, drama by the possibility of some lone summit omitted or, horror of horrors, a change in the sacred tablets. So, if collection is the name of the game and the mountains have run their course, why not change tack and collect something else, such as islands or, more precisely, the islands of Britain? The British Isles!

There is more to this than meets the eye. In the first place there is no definitive list. The collector finds himself in the shoes of Sir H himself. When is an island not an island? When does it merit a place in the list? It may be thought necessary to distinguish islands proper from mere islets, skerries or reefs and to this end a minimum size must be agreed. The 1861 Census defined an island as 'any piece of solid land surrounded by water which affords sufficient vegetation to support one or two sheep'. If this appears too

vague – though much in the spirit of Munro's classi-
fication, allowing your disciples a field day: *Are we
talking Soay Sheep here?* – a minimum area can be stipulated. Forty hectares has been suggested. Even when
this has been agreed, problems loom. Does a bridge
negate island status? Is Skye no more than a penin-
sula? Does Holy Island off the Northumberland coast
cease to be an island when the tide is out? Did the
construction of the Crinan canal create the Isle of
Kintyre and at what cost to the popular music industry? Is Ulster a British Isle? Does the Channel Tunnel undermine the whole concept? The opportunity
for vision and revision is endless.

Given that there are no rules, you can make your
own list. A practical version could include all inhabited islands. There may be more of these than you
think; at the last count there were 61 around Scotland alone. And to keep alive the memories of Munro
days, the landing could only be regarded as completed by the archipelagist ascending the highest
point. In fact, this is to be recommended. If the island is sufficiently small and the summit in question
strategically placed and suitably conical, you can see
with the eye all that appears on the map. You may
find this most satisfactory. It is not often in life that

you know where you stand.

Of all the inhabited British Isles you might choose to visit, there is one which is not likely to spring to mind. That is Rathlin, off the coast of Antrim. In fact, it is the only inhabited British isle off Ireland, the others more renowned in song and drama belonging to the Republic. Its proximity to the Mull of Kintyre makes it almost part of the Inner Hebrides and for centuries there was a running battle as to whether it was Scottish or Irish. Eventually its Irish pedigree was confirmed in 1671 when Sir Randal McDonnell won a law suit at the court of James I. The key piece of evidence was the absence of snakes and toads, a state of affairs apparently peculiar to Ireland alone.

The Rathlin ferry leaves Ballycastle and on a fine day the limestone cliffs glisten, buttressing a land redolent with wrecks and smugglers' coves. A boat trip round the island reveals caves cut into the rock incandescent with reflected light, but the ferry ig- nores such diversions and steams resolutely towards its landing stage in Church Bay. As the harbour ap- proaches, the true shape foreshortened from the mainland is revealed. The island is L-shaped, one side four miles long, the other three and at the three points of the L there is a lighthouse.

The best way to explore the island is to visit each lighthouse in turn. For the most part the island is cultivated and access is restricted to roads and well made tracks. This is not as mundane as it seems. There is no traffic and you are transported to the country lanes of fifty years ago. Banks of primrose, wild violets, kingcups and marsh orchids line the margins. Stonechats, wrens and pippits bob and dart around the hedgerows. Lapwing and oystercatcher strew the fields, whilst lochs and lochans attract a variety of wildfowl.

The simplest and most expedient starting place is McCuaigs Bar and Restaurant. To visit the southern point, follow the road past the Boathouse Visitor Centre and skirt Mill Bay. Both common and grey seals will be found basking on the rocks. On the day we passed we counted over fifty and as each seal will eat two stone of seafood daily the resident population is responsible for the disappearance of a fair few fish suppers. The main road is joined at Soerneog View Hostel where, if speed is of the essence, bikes can be hired. Various lochs are passed and the track peters out at two derelict cottages. Incongruously, one was used for smuggling, the other by the coastguards, apparently in complete harmony. A rough path, part in concrete, can be followed to the lighthouse at Rue Point. Here the mood changes. No longer the peace of the country lane. Waves surge and crash into narrow jagged inlets. Flotsam and jetsam are trapped in crevices and cracks. One such piece of detritus bore the legend DIVERTED TRAFFIC, its arrow pointing optimistically in the direction of the mainland.

The views of the Antrim coast are very fine from this point and well worth a visit. Stubby fingers of headland push into the Sea of Moyle from Fairhead to the Giant's Causeway. One of these headlands is in fact an island, Carrickarede, connected to the mainland by a rope bridge. The passage is only twenty yards long but you are suspended a hundred feet above the sea, which pours at this point through a narrow channel. If windy, the crossing can be an interesting experience. The bridge is put up each spring and taken down each autumn – another poser in the maze of 'when is an island not an island?'

The second and nearest lighthouse to the comforts of Church Bay is at the East Point. There is a loop road that leaves McCuaigs Bar and returns to the village at St Thomas' Church. At its most northern point a track passes through a gate and leads to the East Light. This is the scene of two events that were to change history. Below the lighthouse is a cave that is reputed to be the refuge of Robert the Bruce, where he saw the famous spider continuously trying to spin its web. Inspired by this act of determination in the face of adversity, Bruce returned to Scotland to reclaim his kingdom at Bannockburn. The second event, some six hundred years later, was the transmission of the first radio message by Marconi in Ballycastle to his assistant on Rathlin. He was encouraged in his experiments by the insurers, Lloyds, who had a vested interest in knowing as early as possible whether their ships were safe. Previously, information had been conveyed by carrier pigeon but these too easily fell prey to the raptors that made their home on the crags of Fairhead.

Having taken in the vista of the Mull of Kintyre, which on a good day can look remarkably close, retrace your steps to the road and continue the loop. On your return you will pass the National Trust property of Ballyconagan. This is well worth a visit as it forms a microcosm of the terrain, flora and fauna that comprise the island as a whole.

The West Lighthouse is the furthest from civilisation and the nervous might avail themselves of an occasional minibus service that takes visitors to the

Kebble National Nature reserve and Ireland's largest seabird colony. But it is much better to walk. The road climbs out of the village, past the Church of the Immaculate Conception and a memorial to the five hundred inhabitants who emigrated during the Great Famine, before levelling out to give extensive views both of Church Bay and the Antrim coastline. Slieveanaille (hill of the swan), the highest point on the island, lies just to the north above the Stone Age axe factory which ran a massive European export business four and a half thousand years ago. The purist may wish to visit both. This end of the island seems more rugged and soon ceases to be enclosed, though the lazybeds indicate previous agricultural practice. The fauna also becomes tougher, Irish hares keeping a wary eye for buzzards and peregrine.

The extended road ends at the West Light. This impressive piece of engineering is built into the sheer cliff itself and took seven years to complete. In addition to the road, the project also required the building of a provisioning pier in Cooraghy Bay and a steep cable tramway to the cliff top. Perched above the light itself is the RSPB viewing platform looking down on the sea stacks which provide nesting facilities for thousands of seabirds. Guillemots, kittiwakes, fulmars, razorbills and puffins stake their precarious claim. For the most part they are static but, if something should disturb them and they rise as one, the noise of beating wings is like a roll of thunder. On a calm summer's day this is an impressive spot. In the teeth of winter Atlantic gales it must be awesome.

Nowadays, the Western Lights are unmanned but it was not always so. Keepers were needed to trim and fuel the lamps and groups of lonely men stood between maritime shipping and disaster, a remote chain flashing their pre-arranged signals. Rathlin is at the southern end of the chain, guiding the transatlantic vessels into the ports of Liverpool and Glasgow. At the northern end, twenty-one miles to the west of Lewis, lies a group of rocky isles named after the Christian saint, St Flannan. These were the scene of an annual pilgrimage, which was accompanied by curious conventions. Amongst them, pilgrims were forbidden to relieve themselves near the mooring-place or to kill a bird after sunset and, twenty paces from the altar, were forced to strip off their outer garments. The largest of these islands is Eilean Mór and on it in 1899 the lighthouse was erected which proved to be the scene of a most odd and unsolved mystery.

During the night of 15th December 1900, a pass-

R.S.P.B. West Light
Viewpoint

Bull Point

N

Rathlin Sou

Route Five: Rathlin

East Lighthouse

Harbour

Church Bay.

ud.

Rue Point
Light.

G.R.Dale
Aug '02

ing steamer noted that the light was not working and duly reported the fact. Meanwhile the Hesperus, the lighthouse relief tender, was battling to reach the islands. Hampered by bad weather, it did not arrive until Boxing Day. The crew were surprised that they had no response to the usual signals denoting their arrival and on landing could find no trace of the three keepers. The log book and notes ready to be entered were complete to 9.00 am on the 15th. There was a meal of meat and potatoes on the table but this was untouched. A chair was overturned and the canary was dead in its cage, presumably from malnutrition. Clearly some emergency had occurred for the men to leave in such a hurry. But only two sets of oilskins were missing. Why and at what stage did the third man leave the shelter of the lighthouse unprotected against the elements? If he was in such a hurry, why did he feel it necessary to close not only the door but also the perimeter gate? No satisfactory explanation was ever found and soon the press got tired of stories of sea monsters and ghosts of indignant ancient saints and the affair was forgotten. But there was a curious twist. Towards the end of the century a dramatisation of the events was staged in Glasgow. On that very night the Flannan light, now unmanned, inexplicably went out for only the second time in its history. The date of the production was December 15th.

Even if you don't believe in things that go bump in the night, you have to admit that islands have an air of their own. They are self-contained, separate from the other world. It is no accident that writers of children's fiction make use of such locations. In *Coral Island* it is a vehicle for the various rites of passage that Jack, Ralph and Peterkin have to experience. In Enid Blyton, it allows children to behave in a manner that normally would excite the adult veto. In Arthur Ransome, a mixture of both. Yet only in William Golding's *Lord of the Flies*, a book about, rather than for, children do we see the real truth of island life. There is no place to retreat. No opportunity for the persecuted to drift further west in search of a Terra Nova. You either hid or fought. In addition, since most islanders depend for their existence on the whims of the sea, the winds and the tides, every departure and return must be celebrated. This combination of resolution and fatalism produced a certain type: the Islander who could fend for himself, who, at the same time, welcomed and resisted outsiders, a man with a clear sense of identity. Houses may be empty but there is a held belief that the owners will return. Even in these days of freezers and e-mails, the arrival of the ferry still causes excitement, its delay a concern that is rooted in the old fears at the non-appearance of the fishing fleet. Rathlin hangs on to the school that will ensure its identity, even though there are at present only five pupils and the teacher has to commute from the mainland.

The more remote the island, the more apparent the insularity. By definition, the landmass must be sufficiently small for its inhabitants to be aware of its significance and its particular peril. It is very unlikely that those of Coventry will feel threatened by the cancellation of the Dover Ferry or a local election in East Kilbride. But it is all relative and it's only sixty years ago that happenings as far apart as Scapa Flow and the airfields of south-east England held the attention of a quite large piece of land surrounded by sea. So, maybe the nascent Munro Society has touched a deeper nerve. Donne may well be right when he says that no man is an island and we need to co-exist to be happy. But perhaps we still have an instinctive island mentality, finding it most satisfactory to surround ourselves with a significant sea of like-thinking people who approve of our efforts and give some sort of shape to our ambitions.

Six

One Over The Eight

To suckle fools and chronicle small beer
(Othello)

The eight are the pubs of that number that lie in the parish of Sutton and Sutton is a parish in Macclesfield. The Sutton Eight is a traditional walk that conjoins these pubs. As with all traditions, it goes back as long as is necessary and is satisfactorily vague when it comes to detail. There may well be other versions of the true nature of the event but all this humble researcher can plead is that he asked the question of a participant who not only completed this hazardous enterprise but has also an inscribed glass tankard to prove it. There seems no doubt where it began – with breakfast at the Hanging Gate – and assuming the course is octoliptical, there it must have ended. It is when investigating what happened in between that the memory of the witness tended to slip in and out of focus. So, if the Keeper of the Eight finds the detail to be in error, I apologise in advance. There is amongst walkers, however, a general philosophy that it is better to get more miles than pints under your belt and, given the proximity of pubs in the vicinity of the village of Langley, it is more than probable that these lay towards the end of the course. The longer 'half', to include the Ryles Arms, the Fools Nook and Sutton Hall, is twice as far as the second leg comprising the Lamb Inn, the Church House, the St Dunstan and the Leathers Smithy.

You leave the Hanging Gate either by a path that follows the Rossendale Brook or by joining the Gritstone Trail where it crosses Meg Lane. Both lead to the Ryles Arms and both are Rights of Way. These paths and countless others have a guardian angel in the Peak and Northern Footpaths Society. Every network of paths and bridleways has an inspector who regularly reports on the state of play and any obstruction found is in turn reported by the Society to the relevant local authority. The latter has as much a legal responsibility to maintain the most minor of footpaths as it has to fill in potholes on the A34, but without pressure would undoubtedly allow matters to drift. In addition, the occupier of the land has a variety of tricks to discourage the timid walker.

These fall into three categories, of which the first is the intimidatory approach. In this field there is the possibility of death or serious injury through *(a)* high velocity bullets, *(b)* uncontrolled domesticated animals or *(c)* supposedly controlled sporting spheroids. There is quite properly an outcry when vandals drop lumps of masonry off motorway bridges on to passing BMWs but there are those who would hold that if an owner behaves in like manner on his own land he is entirely within his rights and it is the walker who should beware. Type *(b)* is of current interest. The owner of an estate in north-west Scotland has taken the Beware of the Bull concept a stage further. He proposes to introduce wolves and lynx on to his property to keep the deer population in proper proportion – no doubt with large notices posted at strategic points to this effect. Even if this is not a bluff to deter visitors, I can't see the scheme being very successful. Whilst no expert on the hunting psyche of these particular *ferae naturae*, I would suspect that, having established the average running speed of sheep as opposed to deer, they would happily settle for a diet of lamb over venison. If the aim is to produce a truly effective cull, could he not consider the placing of a machine gun on a suitable bealach and the encouragement of bands of indiscriminate picnickers to drive the beasts in the appropriate direction? At least the tourists could be told where to go (suitable nature trails would suffice) which is more than can be said for the wolves. Purists no doubt will object, claiming a sporting shot rather than indiscriminate massacre is the only way to cull the weak and aged and thus ensure the general well-being of the herd. My only answer is that the wall adornments of Scottish hotels always look as though they were in pretty good shape prior to the moment of their demise and that the collection of twelve pointers is probably less good husbandry and more an adult game of expensive conkers.

The second method is obstruction by default. Examples of this illegal practice are: failing to reconstitute footpaths after ploughing, nailing barbed wire across stiles, or the ambiguous placing of notices relating to electric fences. The worst offender is undoubtedly the slurry lagoon. The farmer finds a suitable dip in the path, fills it with slurry and invites the walker to continue knee-deep if he wishes. An added refinement, encountered on the Southern Upland Way, is to encourage the growth of nettles on the margins between the pool and suitably aggressive barbed wire fencing. Complaints are usually met with some bluster about long-established agricultural custom and practice, with undertones of U Boat blockades and the invasion of substandard food from the Continent. If you attempt to stand your ground, Plan *1(b)* is brought into play in the form of ill-nourished, cross-bred alsatians.

However the third trick is the most insidious. It suggests at first sight that both the landowner and the walker are on the same side and they are acting together for a greater good. The notice, conspicuously discreet, tends to read as follows:

This long-established woodland is the natural habitat of a variety of indigenous flora and fauna and is an area of unique scientific interest. Visitors are requested to leave the path at this point and follow the arrowed diversion.

(A diversion that is usually along an A road belching with juggernauts.) As time passes, the notice is continually toned-up in appearance and content until it reads:

KEEP OUT
Area of Special Scientific Interest as specified by EU Reg 432 (ii)

There are many variants of this, most often concerned with health and hygiene or dangers more apparent than real.

In fact, these problems are greater than is generally realised and it is not only the landlords who are to blame. Local Authorities have let matters slide. It is calculated that nearly £70m is needed to bring the network of paths up to standard and another £18.5m would be needed annually to maintain public rights of way in England and Wales. A recent survey carried out by the Ramblers Association found an average of more than five serious obstructions over each ten kilometres of footpath examined. The Association estimates that a quarter of footpaths in England and Wales are now difficult or impossible to use. Some areas are worse than others. A survey of Norfolk found more than half of the county's 600 footpaths are not properly signposted or not easy to use. I was about to say that in the north west we are luckier, but it is not a matter of luck. It is organisations such as the Peak and Northern that have kept the councils on their toes and we all have a responsibility to help them in their efforts. The RA has a membership of 135,000 and claims that walking ranks as the nation's favourite pastime, with three-quarters of the population taking to the countryside each weekend. If this is true, it looks as if the selfish majority are, as usual, allowing the few to do the hard work.

By now, you should be approaching the Ryles Arms, unassailed, it is to be hoped, by wolf or lynx or (assuming global warming has not advanced too exponentially) packs of marauding polar bears. This is a pleasant enough place, though now more restaurant than pub, and it should not be long before you wish to regain the Gritstone Way and tackle the *mauvais pas* of the circuit – the assault of Croker Hill.

Although there are other footpaths on the west side of Croker Hill, the walker when descending to the Fools Nook feels restricted to the route that passes Hanging Gate Farm and Croker House. Any attempt to cut the corner and descend directly from Fox Bank is actively discouraged and there is no right of way to argue your point. It is because of examples like this that the lobby for the Right to Roam gained voice and promoted the Countryside and Rights of Way Act which, when it comes into effect, will give people a new right to walk over large areas of open countryside and common land. In effect, this covers land that is predominantly mountain, moor, heath or down – that is, land of most interest to walkers and climbers. At first sight this appears very welcome but, as the full title of the Act suggests, there is rather more to it than this. The devil, as usual, is in the detail.

Rights of way are only legitimate if they appear on the Definitive Map as drawn up by the Highway Authority and the Government has merely encouraged, not ordered, the authorities to complete the process of recording historic rights of way in their area. Experience shows that some authorities are less enthusiastic about this than others and if the paths and bridleways are not properly recorded by 2026 they will be extinguished. As it is unlikely that the landowner will be leaping to help, it is the responsibility of the general public to complete the research and take the appropriate legal action. If the active membership of the Peak and Northern is anything to go by, most such enthusiasts are in the twilight of their walking careers and there seems to be little interest amongst the under-fifties. It might well be that a combination of dilatoriness, either accidental or deliberate, could cause important routes of access to be extinguished for ever.

The Act also contains a new right for landowners and occupiers to apply for closure of paths through farmland, woodland or paddocks. In addition, the existing grounds for diversion and closure have been broadened. These new provisions could well be significant. As most areas of open countryside are islands surrounded by cultivated land, they will need rights of way to reach them. If farmers and other land-users exercise their new powers in an uncooperative manner, all sorts of difficulties might arise. One can envisage the Authority solving the problem with a new breed of megaphoned Park Warden bellowing instructions to an ever lengthening queue waiting at the gate of the 'Last Entrance to the Peak District for Fifteen Miles'. In addition, if relations between walker and farmer deteriorate sufficiently, the latter can exercise the right to divert a footpath for fourteen separate days in the year. A judicious choice of dates, coupled with a slurry lagoon alternative, is not beyond the mindset of some whom I have come across.

As always, the problem stems from an understanding of the meaning of the word 'right' and the distinction between 'right' as a universal and immutable state of affairs, as used in the term 'Human Rights', and 'right' as a restricted privilege, as used in the term 'Right of Way'. This confusion explains the apparent contradiction in the sentence issued by the Countryside Agency which reads that *Landowners will have a new right to apply for a right of way to be closed.* If landowners feel that the right of way they have granted out of the kindness of their hearts or, more likely, to provide a speedy way of getting the workers to work, can be enforced in law, they will argue an equal and reciprocal right to use the remainder of their land as they wish and, if necessary, restrict access to others. In short, they will argue that enforcing the new legislation is against natural justice. Each side will have its own agenda, needless and expensive litigation may well occur and that monument to indecision, the Temporary Closure Order, will abound. A simple case of where two rights make a wrong.

There is only one sensible solution if the aim is to give access to the open countryside to everyone, and that is for the country to buy it and manage it for the good of all. There are those who say that the proper course is forfeiture as the land was stolen in the first place, but we live, after all, in an enlightened age and the public purse should pay whatever is the reasonable going price for rock, scrub and heather. In addition, the Highway Authorities should produce and put into practice a plan that allows sensible and varied access through the surrounding areas. There could be rough scrambles for the adventurous and well-laid paths for the disabled. Each would go his own way and erosion and overcrowding would be kept to a minimum.

But do we *really* want access for all or just for those sort of people of whom we generally approve? How many would secretly support 'Fred's Way'? Fred is a fisherman and a lover of the countryside. He believes that all land and their waters should be privately owned and jealously keepered by bucolic bouncers armed with shotguns and rottweilers. In this way only those with sufficient ingenuity, determination or cheek would gain access. It would deter the casual family outing from dumping their litter, the throngs of earnest ramblers yodelling their way up the hillside and the myriad of other offences that Fred finds intrusive and annoying. He would also argue that trespassing gives an edge to the activity, something that is certainly lacking in grinding up and down a featureless Scottish lump to claim Number 232 on the Table of Heights of Less Than Two Thousand Feet on a Cold Day. But whichever view you hold – which, in turn, may have determined your exit point from Fox Bank – you will now, perforce, have joined the old Leek Road which leads to the Fools Nook.

There are various explanations for this curious name, amongst them that it is an innocent or malicious corruption of Charles Oak, a reference to that King's attempt to avoid Cromwell's Ironsides by

Route Six: The Sutton Eight

hiding in a tree. It seems as likely a piece of local history as Robin Hood living in his various eponymous caves, but adds a touch of class to the proceedings. After leaving the pub, the route takes to the canal towpath which it follows to the bridge at Sutton Hall. To keep its level, the canal contours away from the road towards its old adversary, the railway, which it runs alongside in an uneasy truce. This waterway was built in 1831, long after the peak of canal construction. As a result, it never really competed commercially and, not for the last time, speculators in Macclesfield found matters were not exactly as they had hoped.

Towpath walking can become monotonous so, to while away the time, you could contemplate or even practise the sport of canal-jumping. As with golf, this activity originated in Holland and is similarly limited in its ambition. In this case, it consists of jumping across a stretch of water with the aid of a pole. Unlike traditional vaulting, the pole is held towards the middle and, once contact is made with the canal bottom, the participant has to swarm as quickly as possible to the pole's tip, simultaneously shifting his weight to guide his prop towards the other bank. Failure to do either results in, at best, ignominy or, at worst, typhoid. The sport is most keenly contested in Lancashire where at one time it momentarily threatened the supremacy of such hallowed pastimes as rat-catching and League Cricket. But the real experts disdained the Dutch courage of the wooden pole and practised the cabalistic art of cut-hopping. Although the finer points are only known to an inner circle of seasoned veterans, the method is similar to that employed by Barnes Wallis with his bouncing bomb. The cut-hopper jumps the canal but, at the crucial juncture and at, most importantly, one and the same time, puts in a double hitch-kick both to maintain momentum and simultaneously skim off the surface to reach the far bank. There is no doubt that a younger generation weaned on GCSE Physics will cast doubt on the possibility of such a feat, but those of us fortunate enough to have watched Dennis Law in his prime will be less dismissive.

It is probable that the more trepid will cross the canal by bridge no 44 to reach the next port of call. Sutton Hall and the township of Sutton Downes go back a long way. Although it is not mentioned in the Domesday Book, it has had its moments. Sir Richard Sutton was one of the founders of Brasenose College, Oxford, and Raphael Hollinshed, the chronicler whose works lie at the heart of Shakespeare's History Plays, lived within the township. Leave the Hall by a footpath that leads to Lane Ends and the Lamb Inn, and then to Langley. The journey from Sutton to the St Dunstan via the Church House has a certain ecumenical flavour. Sutton Hall was a retreat for persecuted Catholics. Langley was a Wesleyan stronghold, with a pub named after an Archbishop of Canterbury. The Church House no doubt swept up any remaining religious waifs and stray. It would not be wise to get carried away with this idea and make the Lamb over-sacrificial. Although the worst is behind, the remainder is uphill and the path is stony, for there is no real alternative to the road. But it is pleasant enough and at least knows where it is going as it gently strains towards its summit and our final resting place.

Which is more than can be said about Macclesfield which, since my last report, has gone distinctly downhill. Downhill in the sense that the epicentre of weekend revelry has moved from the Olympian heights of the Market Place (reconstructed, at some expense, as a recreational centre for skate-boards) to the depths of Park Green. What were chapels, banks and colleges of learning are now purveyors of liquid amnesia. The last cinema in Macc is a café-bar, a place that during the week resembles an abandoned airport lounge and on Friday night a repository for wild lost souls. But, as with our journey through Sutton, there seems to be a higher purpose at work. If we start with the most up-market, of course only in the topographical sense, there is a natural pilgrimage aided by gravity. First the punters leave Preachers (a disused chapel), pass through the Litten Tree (the gate in churchyards reserved for coffin-bearers) and finish in Purgatory (a purpose-built night club). Whether the Council, careless as to the taxpayers' money, is also constructing a Dante Theme Park by stealth is not clear but I have no doubt that some fearless investigative journalist will unearth the truth in due course. But he will have to be quick. Novelty is all and before time can tell, the loitering heirs will have departed and taken their bacchanalia to Pott Shrigley or, who knows, Whaley Bridge.

Continue along the road from the St Dunstan until a left turn into Holehouse Lane allows the Gritstone Trail to be joined once more just below Teggs Nose. Leave it at the point where a path leads down to a stream, then climbs steeply towards Ridgegate reservoir and thence the Leathers Smithy. These convolutions can simply be avoided by keeping to the road. When you walk through Langley there is a sense that this is a village which exists as a thriving community. A row of small but attractive cottages that are occupied during the week, a frequent bus service into Macclesfield and pockets of local industry support this feeling. Sadly, this is not always the way. In many parts of rural Britain the community has been destroyed by the desire to have a second home, a weekend cottage in the country. Inflated house prices have made it impossible for young locals to buy, and village services decline as the incomers fill up with fuel and food at their nearby hypermarkets. Even weekend cottage is a misnomer. Inclement weather is a quick deterrent and, in the winter, tracts of England, in particular, are cast into outer darkness. There are perfectly acceptable arguments to counter the allegation that 'Property is Theft', but to own more than you reasonably need at the expense of others tends to undermine most of them. Even the pubs suffer. Drink-drive laws demand local customers. If there are no locals, either the pubs close or are turned into restaurants serving microwaved Zebra Steaks & Other Exotics. If any of the indigenous population remains, it is shunted into some convenient corner and force-fed gas corroded beer. The Sutton Eight is, perhaps, less an arbitrary collection of pubs and more a benchmark of how things are. When it becomes the Sutton Three, it may be too late.

To return to the Hanging Gate simply reverse your steps (more obvious in this direction) and rejoin the Gritstone Trail. A better alternative would be to connect with the path that leads into Macclesfield Forest and climb the forest tracks to the boundary wall above Nessit Hill. There used to be a concessionary path that skirted High Moor and joined the walled track that leads to the pub. However, this concession has been withdrawn and a sign erected which suggests, not surprisingly, that the area has been designated by some nebulous European Commission as an area of particular scientific interest. As the terrain would clearly fall into the category of open access, one wonders whether all owners of moorland set aside for the destruction of partially flighted birds will discover the existence of threatened rare sedges that have to be safeguarded for the benefit of future generations. Nevertheless, it is worth continuing by one route or another if only to enjoy, weather permitting, a well earned drink in the beer garden, with its splendid views of much of your travail.

Licensed hostelry has traditionally been at the heart of walking and climbing expeditions, whether it is the Tan Hill Inn and the Cat and Fiddle (the start and finish of a 120-mile long distance jog established in 1952 by members of the Rucksack Club to celebrate their jubilee) or whatever particular Duck 'n' Dive lies at the foot of your favourite gritstone outcrop. Historically the reason is obvious. Mountainous areas were difficult to get to and, having made the effort, it was worth staying a few days. The obvious place to stay, as climbers were traditionally relatively well off, was the local hotel. As a result, certain centres began to establish themselves as *the* place to stay – Pen y Pass and Pen y Gwryd in North Wales, the Sligachan in Skye, Kingshouse and Clachaig, the Scylla and Charybdis (at least to the unwary) of Glen Coe. These were places where information could be garnered and climbing partnerships formed. In the Lake District, the Fell & Rock CC similarly adopted the Sun Inn at Coniston, the Old Dungeon Ghyll in Langdale and, most importantly, the Wastwater Hotel in Wasdale as its various headquarters. Records were kept and libraries formed. The lounge walls were heavy with serious-looking Victorians balancing on one and a half monochromatic tricounis. These were the place to stay. The advent of the motorcycle and tents that kept out the majority of the rain changed matters. Abandoned cottages were resurrected as club huts, barns were surreptitiously enfranchised and the hotel lino that had guarded against mud and various sharp pieces of ironmongery gave way to deep piled carpets and fluttering receptionists. Nevertheless the proprietors, conscious of the economic advantage of courting both tradition and the modern trend, kept the 'Climbers Bar' and replaced the photographs with visions of technicolour lycra on vertical ice. Those of sufficiently advanced age to combine a sense of history with extraneous cash could do worse than indulge in a triangular walking holiday to include these three fine monuments to the past.

But there may be another reason for the popularity of public houses. In my experience, people who walk and climb like to frequent them. Although their chosen activity is essentially individual, it also has a collective streak. Climbing in particular is something you do by yourself with other people. There is a desire to form clubs, compare notes and, under the guise of praising others, pat oneself on the back. *Scalelectron Direct? No, not too bad really now you can get modern gear into the crack on the lip of the overhang. Should be regraded really. We tend to underestimate just how good those guys in the sixties really were.* What better venue than the pub? As the evening lengthens, so ambitions rise. Guidebooks are thumbed with dismissive familiarity. Remembered past triumphs form a life of their own. Distances become longer, rock faces steeper and, spurred by such thoughts, even greater plans are laid. Such is my experience, but perhaps I move in the wrong circles.

Seven

The Doctrine of Descent

Down, thou climbing sorrow,
Thy element's below.
(King Lear)

It was a very pleasant summer's evening. The sort of evening when, if you find the right spot, you can bask away your time thinking of nothing in particular. The spot I had chosen was a small sloping ledge some thirty feet from the ground and the something in particular that I had in my mind was how I should evacuate my present position and, before the sun sank beyond the horizon, relocate in the bar of the pub. This had turned out not to be as simple as I had assumed. To reach my present position, I had traversed across an ever-increasing drop and the final moves to the ledge had required a balanced step up on the right foot, combined with a downward press on smooth rock with the left hand. Once the right leg had straightened, and only then, could a hold be reached which allowed feet to be swapped and the ledge attained. Not particularly difficult when aided by upward motion but rather more precarious in reverse. The way to the top was by a series of mantel-shelves, each, according to the guide book, somewhat more difficult than the last. I had been up and down the first a couple of times, made an unconvincing and unconvinced attempt at the second and been distinctly put off by the apparent lack of holds on the third. Hence the ledge and the ever-setting sun.

I should have known better. Nurtured on dire warnings against solo climbing by men who knew a thing or two, I recollected from my formative reading an article in an early *Fell & Rock Journal*. It was on the subject of climbing down, written by Siegfried Herford, the first ascensionist of Central Buttress on Scafell, for many years the hardest climb in Britain. The descent of steep rock, according to Herford, was a question of balance, and balance

> *consists largely in an instinctive anticipation of the effect which a given change of one's attitude will have on the general equilibrium.*

I felt this more or less summed up why Herford, at this moment, would be enjoying a glass of beer and I was stuck on a ledge. I also had time to ruminate on my reasons for climbing and their relationship to the true nature of hubris. Was I only really interested in ticking the book, dropping the name? In which case the fall that might follow this particular form of pride was somewhat more than metaphorical.

What really complicated matters was that I had a choice. Not reversing the traverse – the anticipation of the effect on the general equilibrium had long scuppered that. It was the presence of a corner-cum-gully that lay a few yards to my right that was causing the dilemma. I had discovered that by leaning off the arête I could just reach a thin crack in the adjoining wall. Jamming the fingers of my right hand into the crack, I might scrabble across the rock face and, using the momentum of the induced pendulum, jump for a grassy ledge from which descent would be a formality. This was my favoured plan but there were a couple of drawbacks. First, I might not reach the ledge (I tried to recall the technical detail of how Don Whillans allegedly descended such corners at Stanage by bounding from wall to wall) and, second, my fingers, jammed with cowardly ferocity, might, when weight was applied, find themselves inextricably stuck. The light of the sun diminished in due proportion to the brightening of the lamps in the valley.

So it was to be upward, ever upward. It is suggested in certain quarters that at times of challenge one should recall past triumphs and, thus inspired, step boldly forth, etc. The only occasion I could recall that resembled the present was on an ill-considered cliff in Skye. There I was belayed on the lip of an overhang and my leader was above me in the mist explaining that somehow we had lost the route. The proof of this was the amount of loose rock which suggested uncharted territory and that the last few moves had been a damned sight harder than 'mild severe in dry conditions'. My helpful remarks that the mist probably made a difference were ignored. The leader and some of the loose rock descended. The latter would slither down the slab, clip my ledge and, some thought-provoking seconds later, echo hollowly in the corrie below. The former, fortunately, given the fragility of the belay, did not.

In the end, I did the three mantelshelves and, as usual when you get going, you find there is really nothing to it.

The point of the story is not to denigrate solo climbing or even outdoor gymnastics (*vid sup* C E Benson in Chapter One) but to examine the need for the serious hill walker to ascend or, more particularly, descend relatively steep but technically easy rock. By serious hill walker, I mean someone who intends to climb Scottish mountains in the summer months. It is accepted that, if you exclude the Islands, there is no hill in Scotland that requires rock climbing skills to attain its summit, though the Cobbler might challenge this assertion. Nevertheless, an error of judgement or force of circumstances could mean that the walker might find himself in a position where the ability to climb up or down would be important. It would therefore seem sensible that the serious hill walker should feel comfortable enough to solo the lowest technical rock climbing grades, as without this accomplishment he could get himself into as much trouble as walking in winter without ice-axe and crampons. Even if the rocks are easy, climbing down often needs to be done at speed, particularly when the days are short. Herford, again, has no doubts as to the general competence of his contemporaries:

> To start off with, the 'face-out' method is too seldom adopted; then, too little use is made of gravity and friction; the whole progression from one hold to the next is too calculated and exact, and each individual hold, instead of being regarded as a mere incident in one continuous passage, too often appears to mark, as it were, the end of one section and the beginning of

Route Seven: An Alternative Snowdon Horseshoe

G.K.Dale Aug '06

> *another. The only remedy for this, as with all faults,*
> *is practice.'*

This may have been written nearly a hundred years ago but is no less true today and, as a crisis is rarely the best place to learn, spending some time ascending and descending the easier routes of your local outcrop and learning how to handle a rope could well pay dividends.

But there is a dimension other than safety that is open to the hill walker who can climb a bit. This is the area known as scrambling. Particularly in ascent, the boring plod can be replaced by linking together rocky outcrops and bands of slabs. This is especially true of Scotland, where rock is never far from the surface, and in the Lochaber district alone seventy scrambles have been described and published, ranging from the straightforward, where the difficulties are short and usually avoidable, to serious undertakings with continuous exposure, poor rock or difficulty of retreat. Nearly all lead to or near the top of the hill, most of which are Munros or Corbetts. The Munroist who climbs Meall Dearg or Sgorr nam Fiannaidh as separate entities rather than connecting them via the Aonach Eagach Ridge is rather missing the point. Munro did not see his eponymous mountains and tops as separate expeditions but rather as particular landmarks in a day's mountaineering, and plodding up and down the fringes of Clachaig Gully to add another number to your list bears no comparison to a day that starts at the Am Bodach and finishes at the Pap of Glencoe. In fact, serious scramblers would start from 'The Study' and include a route on A'Chailleach.

Further north, the classic peaks of Liathach and An Teallach offer much more to those who are prepared to stay on the ridge rather than scuttle round the difficulties, and many of the rocky outbursts of Sutherland are only accessible to those who are happy to use their hands and accept a degree of exposure. But it is the ridges of the Islands to which the serious hill walkers should aspire. The best known is the Cuillin on Skye and, even if the continuous traverse is beyond them, the attempt to complete it in pieces should be contemplated. In this way, they could, if they wished, avoid the more difficult passages, *ie* the crossing of the Thearlich Dubh gap, the traverse of Bidean Druim nan Ramh and the ascents of the Inaccessible Pinnacle and the Basteir Tooth. It might be wiser to try the hills of Rhum and Arran first. These give some idea of the problems involved in a long ridge scramble. If, on the latter, you can manage the descent from A'Chir and the traverse of the Witch's Step without qualm, then most of the Cuillin ridge should be within your grasp.

There are good long scrambles to be had outwith Scotland and it is generally assumed that the best expedition in North Wales is the Snowdon Horseshoe. But after Crib y Ddysgl the whole thing peters out and the only real danger that remains is being run over by a train. With a little more ambition, the hill walker with limited rock climbing skills could fashion a round which is not only superior but somewhat less cluttered with empty cans of coke. It also has three peaks over three thousand feet and is considerably longer and more challenging than the Horseshoe. The key is the successive bands of rock that run down from the summit plateau of Glyder Fawr. Start in Cwm Idwal and climb the Slabs by the Ordinary Route, an easy-angled furrow that leads to the Terrace below Holly Tree Wall. There are no easy routes here but it can be turned without difficulty on the left to another more commodious terrace below Continuation Wall. Here, an enjoyable scramble up a staircase-like break connects with a series of walls and slabs that can be joined together at random. This eventually reaches Seniors' Ridge, which forms the edge of the Upper Cliff of Glyder Fawr and leads to the summit. The plateau is crossed to Glyder Fach which is descended in the direction of Bristly Ridge (all this can be quite tricky in mist and can add to the fun). Descend the ridge to Bwlch Tryfan. From here, traverse the third peak, Tryfan, by the most distinctive skyline in Britain. As a neat complement to the Idwal Slabs, the day could finish with the descent of one of the easier routes on Milestone Buttress, though this would produce something of a sting in the tail. None of this is technically difficult but it is a serious undertaking and it would be wise for a party to carry a rope and a few nuts and slings. In fact, this is true of all mountain excursions where they might be needed to inspire confidence or assist a judicious retreat.

So what about that other mountainous area of Britain, the Lake District? At first sight this does not seem so promising. The cliffs tend to be discrete lumps of rock perched on the hillside and there are no ridges to compare with Wales or Scotland. The obvious scrambling day is the ascent and descent of Pillar Rock by its easiest routes, but, impressive as it is, it is a long way to walk for a few hundred feet of climbing. There are other passages that require the use of hands but they tend to be short or easily avoidable. And so it may have well remained if it had not been for the efforts of Bentley Beetham. He turned the traditional concept of climbing on its head and, instead of climbing a weakness in otherwise impregnable rock, he sought out difficult ways up easy ground.

Beetham was a teacher at Barnard Castle School and in 1936 the Goldsborough Club, the mountaineering activity at the school, acquired the lease of a hut near Rosthwaite in Borrowdale. In Beetham's opinion, 'if boys were to be suitably introduced to the true joys and art of mountaineering, the popular crags would have to be eschewed.' He gave an example of a visit to Great Gable in the hope that most holiday visitors would have departed:

> On arrival at the Napes we found more than seventy people festooned on and about the Needle and the Dress Circle. Had we required an insight into the management of a circus or of a performing-flea show it might have been useful, but as an introduction to mountaineering it was utterly repellent.

He therefore set about unearthing, usually literally, rock faces covered in vegetation and hidden by trees. Eventually he was able to report to the Fell & Rock CC that Borrowdale, previously dismissed as being of little or no interest to its members, had in fact 20,000 feet of climbing within a radius of two miles. When the new guidebook came out, his additions had a mixed reception. Many routes were not obvious and defied a straightforward topographical description. Climbers, having spent an afternoon trying to locate The Higher The Better or Ant Highway amongst a plethora of boulders and frondescence, or bewildered by such route descriptions as 'an ascent had been made but no route had been found', were quick to disparage his efforts as pointlessly artificial. A later generation went further and suggested that the harder climbs had been done through binoculars rather than by legitimate means. Both these criticisms were unfair. Beetham was an outstanding rock climber and mountaineer. He completed the second ascent of Central Buttress on Scafell and was a member of the 1924 Everest expedition. There is no doubt that he had the technical competence and *sang froid* to complete all the climbs he claimed as solo ascents. With regard to the criticism of artificiality, that he merely linked small outcrops separated by swathes of easy ground, it must be remembered that his original aim was to find rock pitches which were suitable for youthful beginners. As a responsible professional,

he made sure that the situations were not over-in-
timidating and, if necessary, that they could be abandoned if found too taxing. He also defends them from
another viewpoint. Unlike the classic courses which
are spread out before the climber, his Borrowdale
climbs, he explains,

> *have to be found, identified and* carefully followed.
> *In this last there is a hidden virtue, useful as train-*
> *ing for the Alps, where a slight deviation from the*
> *intended route may lead one to an impasse, to less*
> *interesting climbing, or to a wrong destination alto-*
> *gether.*

Indeed, he may have had greater aspirations for his
protégés than joining the crag-rats that now infest the
base of his greatest discovery, Shepherd's Crag.
Names like 'Mountain Way' and 'Rabbit's Trod' suggest a search for higher planes and he worked out
long routes that started in the valley and finished after a thousand feet or so on the high fells with a day's
walking in front of you. At the very least, he proved
it is possible to climb familiar hills without joining a
queue at every impasse. But he must have gone further than that and hit a nerve with the general climbing public, as bookshelves of *Scrambles in Wherever
You Can Think Of* clearly attest.

As the chapter started with the vicissitudes of solo climbing, perhaps it would be appropriate to examine the merits or otherwise of walking alone. The downside is fairly clear: a fall which results in an inability to move would mean considerable inconvenience to others and, at worst, might prove fatal. Dave Hewitt, in his account of walking the Scottish Watershed, describes such a moment:

I had stepped out on a secure-looking grass ledge which gave way, sending me head-first plummeting rolling jolting, arms and legs flailing, some ten twenty thirty metres to a juddering halt among mud and rocks below. I lie there winded, dazed, glasses gone, aware only of blurred outlines of hills and a warm drip-drip of blood down my shirt to tell of still being alive. [...] Then a vicious self-anger takes hold and my head begins to throb — more with frustration at my own stupidity than with any great pain. I heard myself repeating and repeating, as though spoken by someone else, the words 'Shit' and 'God help me'. Skewed and sprawled and shaking on the hillside, the name of the game is no longer Watershed, but Survival.

However, the dangers of dying through malnutrition can be mitigated by carrying a mobile phone, whistle, or even emergency flares, and there have been cases when people have survived for considerable periods of time. In 1921 a Mr Crump from London decided to walk from Coniston to Wasdale Head. He lost his way and tried to reach his objective by climbing down Piers Gill, a deep rift of waterfalls that separates Great End from Lingmell. The summer had been unusually dry and he was able to descend a series of pitches that were then free of water. On the last of these he fell and was badly injured. Although Baddeley, the walker's guide, describes the Gill as a way to reach Scafell Pike, the description is cloaked with stern warnings and at that time the Gill had only been climbed twice, on both occasions by parties of men wearing bathing suits. So the search parties, though out on the fells for days, failed to consider it as a possible route. Some weeks later and encouraged by the continuing fine weather, a party of three decided to attempt the first descent of the Gill and found Mr Crump apparently resting in its bed and gazing down the ravine. He had been there twenty days and twenty nights without food or shelter. The climbers lowered him over further difficulties and transported him to Wasdale, where he made a complete recovery. Only a considerable slice of fortune and a ready supply of water had saved him. But no matter how careful or lucky you are, rocks fracture and heather can cover a multitude of hidden traps. There is no doubt that walking in the mountains can be dangerous and walking by yourself must increase the odds of something irremediable happening.

But the skill and pleasure of mountaineering is moving safely in dangerous places and there is a particular satisfaction in navigating a tricky mist-covered passage or completing an awkward descent before an October darkness falls. This sense of satisfaction is heightened if you alone have overcome the problems. And the real plus of walking by yourself is that you see so much more. First out in the morning catches a variety of worms, largish mammals calling it a night, raptors sitting on gateposts planning the day's campaign and a variety of small furry animals scurrying for cover. All these add colour to the margins of the mountain day, less often experienced by a small party and rarely by a regimented group of the local ramblers' association. There is no doubt that, in the balance of common sense, solitary walking or climbing will be found wanting, but I think I got more out of a late evening climb on the Roaches than I did from much harder climbs secured by a rope.

Eight
Coasting Home

Here is my journey's end, here is my butt,
And very seamark of my utmost sail.
(Othello)

I have mentioned elsewhere that I prefer the route from A to B to the circular version. With the latter, until a certain point, it is as easy to return as to go on and the nature of the enterprise means that the second half can often be considerably avoided. This option is not so readily available on the linear path; when you have left A, if you are to make any progress, you have to keep going until B hoves into view. Circularists would argue that this alternative is equally artificial. Why start at A? Why finish at B? What is so sacrosanct about Marsden or Edale? Well, train stations for a start but that's another story. But they would find it hard to quibble when A is on one side of the country and B is on the other and the only alternative is getting your feet wet. So, the ideal linear path is a coast-to-coast. Hill walkers in Britain are fortunate in this respect. Nowhere is it extraordinarily wide and many of the narrower parts are mountainous.

The choice is various and a matter of taste – not that I would recommend Milford Haven to Felixstowe via Swindon and Milton Keynes.

The man who is credited with the coast-to-coast concept or, at least, who put it on the map is Alfred Wainwright. Although his contribution to the development of mountaineering is modest, there is no doubt that his effect on hill walking, particularly in the Lake District, is anything but. His collection of maps, sketches and guided tours represents a lifetime's work and demonstrates a knowledge of the hills and moors of the North of England that is probably unrivalled. What drove the man to the lengths he took is difficult to explain but Hunter Davies's sympathetic biography is revealing. There is no doubt that, in the language of his day, he was an odd cove. Whether this had anything to do with his being, as a red-haired baby, locked in a drawer when the household received visitors, is difficult to say. But whatever the cause, he grew into a man who became increasingly isolated from his friends and family, locking his personal life in a secret drawer of his own.

It was perhaps to avoid addressing the realities of his ill-chosen marriage that he set himself the task of first climbing and second drawing every route up every fell in the Lake District. This activity allowed him to spend the weekends out of the house and the evenings in the privacy of his study. The outcome was a meticulous extravagance of words and drawings that, in seven volumes, laid out for all to see the high land that lies within the National Park. At first sight, they must have appeared little more than a curiosity, a series of books that showed more of an insight into the workings of a man's mind than a useful addition to the canon of Lakeland mountaineering literature. After all, at the time when he started his opus those who roamed the high fells were either professional locals or capable walkers and climbers who needed no recourse to step-by-step accounts. Not obvious hot cake material. But sell they did and in copious numbers. It was not even as though they sprang from the board of particular expertise. Wainwright had no knowledge of the nature of printing and publishing and assumed, with much waste, that his written words and drawings must fit exactly on to the page. His publisher was a local newspaper and the sales distribution took the form of him and his publisher touring the small bookshops of the district in the hope that they might be persuaded to stock a few copies.

Word of mouth alone led to reprint after money-spinning reprint. It is interesting to speculate whether this could happen today. In times of pile 'em high and sell 'em cheap, the bookselling chainstores control not only public taste but, what is worse, the discerning booksellers who used to be willing to stock the odd title that might catch the eye of the browser. In turn, small publishers, punished by extortionate discounts, are understandably wary of anything that has not already an established market niche. Perhaps, in those days, the local bookseller, like the local grocer, kept in touch with his customers' interests. Perhaps they were more aware than the chief accountants of what was happening on the ground.

What is more, in the late fifties and early sixties a new breed of walker appeared. They were not the same as the pre-war band who escaped to the hills to avoid the smoke and poverty of the industrial cities. They were better off, more mobile and with more leisure time. Jobs were secure and, so the politicians told them, they had never had it so good. People could afford to buy boots for recreation rather than work. There were some, of course, who wanted to find out for themselves, but many needed a little push to get them started. Wainwright's books offered just

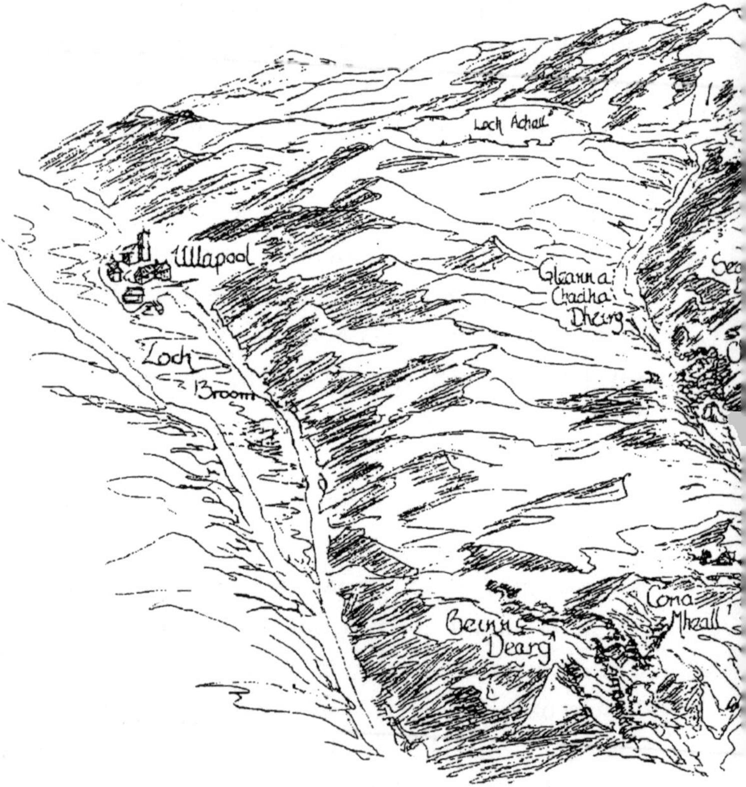
Loch Achall
Ullapool
Glearn a Chadha Dheirg
Loch
Broom
Beinn Dearg
Cona Mheall

Route Eight: A Scottish Coast-to-Coast

Knoidaruph

Carn Ban

Bonar Bridge

Alladale

Strathcarron

Gleann Mor

Glenbeg

G.R. Dove   Aug '02

such encouragement. They suggested that there was, if not a legal, at least a moral right to wander round on other people's property and that the paths the town dweller saw leaving the safety of the metalled road would lead him not to the edge of some awful abyss but deliver him safely to the summit of the hill of his choice. So their confidence in the author as mentor increased as he offered sensible ways of avoiding the tricky bits and treated them not as novices to be patronised but as equals to be encouraged. The knock-on, or perhaps knock-down, effect was considerable. As a result of this friendly shoulder, paths delineated by Wainwright were slavishly followed and worn to shreds. Delicate sheep trods became deep ruts of earth, grassy slopes were eroded into bare brown motorways, scree slopes polished into bald skating rinks.

Of course, it wasn't his fault. He couldn't have foreseen the impact and, as I have suggested, there were many other influences at play. If he hadn't done it, someone else would. However, there is a lesson to be learnt. Guide books should suggest generalities rather than lead by the hand. To plot your own Lake District route distinguishes you from the herdwicks. To use a map and compass is not only rewarding but, if you were to stray from the primrose path, is also as good a way as any to prevent the lost sheep from stepping over that bourne from which no traveller returns. This is what lies behind the right to roam. It doesn't mean the right to demolish drystone walling or invade people's privacy. It means the right to choose which way you want to go. To reach England's highest mountain not by following the security blanket of cairns via Esk Hause but rather, if you so choose, by Cust's Gully and the rocky escarpment of Great End.

But the floodgates had opened. Each reprint dug doubly deep and, buoyed by his success and transported by an at last found love, Wainwright cast his net ever wider. Using the same format, he set out to plot the Pennine Way. There is no doubt that he felt this, if not a waste of time, was a far remove from his beloved Lakes. Indeed, he arranged for any walker who had the bloody-mindedness to finish the thing to be rewarded with a free drink on arrival at Kirk Yetholm. Nevertheless, its popularity persuaded him to undertake another long distance route, but this time one of his own making. So there came about the coast-to-coast from St Bees Head to Robin Hood's Bay. Prudence dictated a west-east crossing, treating the prevailing wind as a friend rather than an enemy. This turned out to be a partial mistake as the walk had, at least to the author, a sense of anti-climax. The North Yorkshire Moors do not measure up to the Lakeland Fells and the trudge across the boring flatness between Richmond and the A19 was not alleviated by the thought of things to come.

As coast-to-coasts go, it wasn't the first by a long way. Both Offa's Dyke and Hadrian's Wall followed the same principle, if for rather different reasons. Both, as you would expect, are now long distance footpaths, with their accompanying instruction manual. Britain's first 'official' coast-to-coast footpath is the Southern Upland Way. This is very much a curate's egg. It starts well enough along interesting sea cliffs but the next fifty miles or so to Bargrennan contain too much road work and all too similar forest rides. The next fifty are rather different. The scenery is more rugged, distances between accommodation are greater and Glen Trool and its surrounding hills have their particular charms. Mist over moorland requires care but it was the depths of the Galloway Forest that gave the real cause for concern.

Although I didn't know it at the time, my hip problem was beginning to manifest itself. This meant I was walking somewhat more slowly than my wife. Judicious map inspection and looming mist kept the party together but when the going got easier along macadam or, in this case, a forest road, Tricia would tend to surge ahead. This presented no real difficulty as it accommodated the obligatory tea stops in a satisfactory manner. I had temporarily lost sight of her around a bend so was surprised to find her stopped in her tracks. *There's a man hiding behind that tree!* was the accompanying theatrical whisper to guarded gesticulation. At that moment a largish figure appeared, draped in a scruffy overcoat, unshaven, dishevelled and with a face twisted into half smile, half grimace. He gave the appearance of a misplaced beggar whose normal milieu was the London Underground. Galloway Forest is very large. It was midweek and we had seen no other walkers. *Just keep walking* was the lord and masterly injunction. After a hundred yards or so, when the miraculous cure for arthritic hips had worn off, the pace slowed. As the Madman from Merrick seemed to have gone about his business, we were just thinking of stopping for lunch, when from a nearby forest ride appeared two equally burly men similarly garbed and tonsured, one of them, rather worryingly, carrying a three-quarter empty bottle of whisky. The question/statement/threat that one of the pair uttered I answered in a manner that tried to appear simultaneously dismissive yet conciliatory and we sped on with the aid of another visitation from Lourdes. Lunch was forgotten. Even the obligatory tea stop was shelved until the trees were cleared and habitation was in sight.

It was only in the bar that night that we discovered the truth. The army had at the beginning of the week released a bunch of new recruits on a survival course into the Forest. Their brief was to last the week without being 'captured' and to live off the land as best they could. Apparently the consequences of being caught were worse than their current deprivations. The providentially found whisky bottle contained nothing more sinister than peaty water and the question/statement/threat was probably a polite request for any spare sandwiches which we might have lying around the bottom of our rucksacks.

The remainder of the journey was not so dramatic. The Border country from Wanlockhead, the highest village in Scotland, where they still pan for gold, and on to Lauder offers rolling, spacious walking and the stops prove interesting, none more so than Tibbie Sheil's Inn, an oasis in an otherwise remote area.

Tibbie lived from 1782-1878 and her reputation as an innkeeper persuaded such luminaries as Sir Walter Scott and James Hogg, the Ettrick Shepherd, to adopt the place for their literary soirées. Moffat is nice but Melrose is better and although, as you would expect, the whole affair falls away towards the end, there is usually something to catch your interest in the manner of abbeys, castles and bridges. For the less experienced, it is best done in pieces; even the long hauls can be broken down by hoteliers who are willing to shuttle their guests hither and thither. For the more experienced, it's best to get out the map and just do the good bits.

But if you are looking for the ultimate coast-to-coast, look no further than the stretch between Bonar Bridge and Ullapool. As the crow flies, it is less than fifty miles and is in the only area of Britain where you can go from one side of the country to the other without crossing a main road. (Wainwright's effort, for example, has to navigate a passage across, *inter alia,* both the M6 and the A1.) The route passes through one of the most remote parts of the Highlands – if you don't see a Golden Eagle you're unlucky – and offers a variety of ways to suit all tastes. You could run through it in a day. You could spend a week or so collecting mountains in the way that others collect stamps and, to save the fag of carrying a tent, there is not one but three bothies, Alladale, Glenbeg and Knockdamph, situated on route.

A bothy is a simple structure that withstands wind and rain and was traditionally used to shelter shepherds and ghillies or to save an often lengthy journey between home and workplace. In more recent time, the maintenance of these buildings has, with the approval of the landowner, been taken on by the Mountain Bothies Association. The self-appointed task of the members is to keep the place dry and relatively warm. To that end, there is a roof and a fireplace and, in addition, often a sleeping platform (to separate the men from the mice) and table or bench for cooking and eating. Many contain no more than one room while others, like Ben Alder with its ghost and Shenevall with its stunning views, have a structure that suggests permanent residency in former times. But they are all freely available and there is no membership. Their primary function is to provide shelter and so save lives, the secondary to give walkers and climbers a convenient base to tackle the routes on a remote crag or 'collect' a significant number of tops in a day.

It is this dual function that has caused the Association its biggest headache and the greatest difference of opinion between members. Do you or do you not advertise the bothy's presence, giving grid references and routes of access? If you don't, the beleagured could die not knowing that shelter was within easy reach. If you do, they become hotels. Well, not what the average person calls a hotel, though the bothy at Tarf does have an affixed AA approval sign, complete with stars, but somewhere that offers accommodation. This would not matter if the party numbered two or three, but the problem comes when led groups of students and the like invade the premises. I once visited Shenevall to find it occupied by what appeared to be a large slice of NATO's strategic defence force and was faced with the alternative of a particularly decrepit and odorous lean-to or sharing an already cramped vestibule. I have no problem with the romantic notion of sleeping under the stars. It's when there aren't any that I get fussy. A more serious problem is with the more accessible bothies. These are often taken over, not by climbers but a gang on a night out from a nearby town or city. The proximity of bothy to off-licence means at best a rowdy night, at worst considerable unpleasantness.

There is inevitably vandalism, mostly in the destruction of anything combustible to fuel the fire, but at times it is wanton, laying waste in minutes the labour of hours. On top of all this, the Association faces problems of Health and Safety, Incorporation and the like. The older members must think it a far cry from the day when a few lads got together to repair the roof of a hut so that they could spend a few more hours on that big crag behind it.

The bothies on this route are still a bit too far north to have much trouble, although there is the usual problem of people being too idle to take away their rubbish. All over Scotland there is a plethora of whisky bottles left 'in case any one wants to use them as a candle holder'. But if you are a collector of mountains you will find bothies with or without rubbish most helpful and, as the outward journey is not particularly arduous, you might even consider taking the superfluous glassware with you. Although the route is in a remote part of Britain, Bonar Bridge is served by a train which connects at Inverness with the sleeper from the south. There is also an efficient bus service from Ullapool to Inverness, so the interminable drive north can easily be avoided. The simplest route is a low level stroll along the estate tracks of Gleann Mór and Gleann Beag, over the bealach at Cadha Dearg to join another track at East Rhidorrach Lodge, and then by Glen Achall to Ullapool. Here you may or may not pass the odd pub or two before paddling in the sea. This would be an easy enough three-day walk. Unless it rains. The streams rise quickly hereabouts. I can remember boulder-hopping across the foot of a stream one sunny evening, then having to climb several hundred feet of mountain to find a suitably shallow crossing point the next morning.

However, if you are lucky and can spend a week of perfect pre-midge weather in May or early June, you can hang around for a few days and collect Tops by the cartload. There are six Munros, tops over 3000 feet, four Corbetts, over 2500 feet, and six (more if you push it) Grahams, over 2000 feet. Of course, these are now measured in metres but, whatever sanctions Brussels may eventually impose, I cannot see the expression 'threethousander' disappearing. A 'thousand-meterer' doesn't have quite the same ring. If time is short, Beinn Dearg is a must. It can be ascended directly from Glenbeg bothy via Loch Prille and the rocky ridge of Cona Mheall. In addition, the Munros Meall nan Ceapraichean and Eididh nan Clach Geala can more easily be included in the round than

155

pronounced. I would also suggest you pick up Seana Bhraigh and the Corbett, Bodach Mor, while you're there. It is, as I found out to my cost, a long way back from Macclesfield for just one mountain. When you reach the summit of Seana Bhraigh, you find you have reached the edge of the Highlands. There are many more and indeed finer mountains further north but these have erupted from a lowland plain. The high-lands proper is a plateau starting in the east at 4000 feet and shelving gently to 3000 feet in the west. Time and natural forces have broken this landmass into valleys and peaks but in essence it is all of a piece. As this is the true edge of Munro country and the end of the tick list, the aspirant should look north, for there is the promised land – hills more noted for their elegance than their vital statistics. Not a mel, meall or meallach among them!

Even if it is not from coast to coast, I especially enjoy a walk that finishes where the land meets the sea, and when this happens I sometimes think of the man who took his young daughter for a walk. They had taken a bus and intended to return up the glen, over the bealach, then down the other side in time for tea. It wasn't too far and in good weather, with visits to waterfalls and gatherings of flowers, there seemed little in the way of a problem. The forecast said it would stay fair, but the people who make the forecast live in London or places where the weather does much as it's told. This part of the world has a climate of its own dictated by the mountains and the turnings of the tide. So, when the air suddenly started to move he became anxious. Short bursts pulled at the vegetation. The temperature dropped. It was a long way to go back, even if there were a bus. He should have checked. At first the child saw nothing. But the increase in pace and the impatience at dawdling began to communicate the man's anxiety. There wasn't that much to climb, just two or three hundred feet of rock and rough heather. If it had been sunny they could have scrambled from outcrop to outcrop but by now the mist had fallen and the rock was wet and cold and the heather roots clutched at boots and wellingtons. A few hundred feet and they would reach the good track that led down to the harbour where soup and congratulations would be offered in appropriate proportion.

To busy her mind from what she now saw as an outrageously miserable chore, the man told the child the story of Xenophon, a soldier and writer from Athens, who, after the death of his king in battle, had to lead ten thousand Greeks back from the middle of Persia to the coast whence they could sail to their homelands. He cheered up his men by telling them stories and, despite attacks from ferocious mountain tribes and all the frost and snow and ice that the Armenian mountains could throw at them, he led his army 1500 miles to safety. The man had forgotten the historical detail but what he couldn't remember he made up or borrowed from other stories. For he had to spin it out so the end of the tale was reached at the right point on the ground. Near enough to the top to encourage anticipation, not so far as to doubly dash anticipated hopes. That is because the story ends when, at the moment it seems that even Xenophon's efforts will fail, there is a faint cry from a group sent ahead to trudge up yet another unending slope of shifting rock and barren stone. A cry that hangs in the air – θαλαττα, θαλαττα – the sea! the sea! Like the sea itself, the words surged through the ranks – θαλαττα, θαλαττα – and with swords beating on their shields they stormed the slope to be the first to gaze on the waves and the ships that would carry them home.

The man and the child stood on the good track looking down at the harbour and the converted blackhouse with smoke rising straight from the chimney. The wind had dropped and the mist was lifting. The islands in the bay rode at anchor, wet rock catching the unstressed glint of the late autumn sun. The child tore off the anorak hood which had previously turned her face into an oval of woe and, picking up a rock, pitched it into a puddle with a thoroughly satisfactory splash.

Bibliography

Angell, S: *Pinnacle Club. A History of Women Climbing* (Pinnacle Club, 1988)

Benson, C E: *British Mountaineering* (Routledge & Sons, 1909)

Berry, N F: *The Wilson Run. The First 100 Years* (privately printed)

Davies, H: *Wainwright. The Biography* (Michael Joseph, 1995)

Dodd, A E and E M: *Peakland Roads and Trackways* (Landmark Publishing, 2000)

Ginesi, J E: *The Yorkshire Dales Centurion Walk* (J Siddall Ltd, Cleckheaton)

Haswell-Smith, H: *Scottish Islands* (Canongate Books, 1996)

Hewitt, D: *Walking the Watershed* (TACit Press, 1994)

McCurdy, A: *Rathlin's Rugged Story* (Impact Printing, 2000)

Moffat, G: *Space Below My Feet* (Hodder & Stoughton, 1961)

Moir, D G: *Scottish Hill Tracks* (The Scottish Rights of Way Society & Scottish Mountaineering Trust, 1995)

Perrin, J: *Mirrors in the Cliffs* (Diadem Books, 1983)

Pilley, D: *Climbing Days* (Secker & Warburg, 1935)

Smith, R: *The Southern Upland Way* (HMSO, 1994)

Smith, R: *The Winding Trail* (Diadem Books, 1981)

Wainwright, A: 'A Coast to Coast Walk' (*Westmorland Gazette*, 1973)

Williams, N: *Scrambles in Lochaber* (Cicerone Press, 1985)

Xenophon: *Anabasis* (c 390 BC)